D0479308

microgreengarden

mark mathew braunstein

Book Publishing Company
Summertown, Tennessee

Library of Congress Cataloging-in-Publication Data

Braunstein, Mark Mathew, 1951-
    Microgreen garden : indoor grower's guide to gourmet greens / by Mark Mathew
Braunstein.
        p. cm.
    Includes index.
    ISBN 978-1-57067-294-1 (pbk.) — ISBN 978-1-57067-899-8 (e-book)
  1. Edible greens. 2. Indoor gardening. 3. Container gardening. 4. Gardens,
Miniature. I. Title. II. Title: Indoor grower's guide to gourmet greens.
    SB339.B68 2013
    635'.3—dc23

                                                                    2013002999

*Cover photos, top to bottom: Sorrel, Marjoram,
and Sesame (front); Cinnamon Basil and Romaine
Lettuce (back)*

Cover and interior design: John Wincek
Stock photography: 123 RF

Printed in Hong Kong

Book Publishing Company
P.O. Box 99
Summertown, TN 38483
888-260-8458
bookpubco.com

ISBN 13: 978-1-57067-294-1

19 18 17   4 5 6 7 8 9

Book Publishing Company is a member of
Green Press Initiative. We chose to print this
title on paper with 100% postconsumer
recycled content, processed without chlorine,
which saves the following natural resources:

        29 trees
        908 pounds of solid waste
        13,575 gallons of water
        2,502 pounds of greenhouse gases
        13 million BTU of energy

For more information on Green Press Initiative,
visit greenpressinitiative.org.

Environmental impact estimates were made
using the Environmental Defense Fund
Paper Calculator. For more information visit
papercalculator.org.

Printed on recycled paper

CONTENTS

ACKNOWLEDGMENTS

This book is for people who want to grow microgreen gardens at home, but in writing it, I've drawn from the expertise of professional growers. I owe my thanks to Lauri Roberts of Farming Turtles Microgreens, based in Exeter, Rhode Island. Lauri graciously guided me on a tour of her indoor microgreen farm and showed me how to grow microgreens affordably, cleanly, and easily.

The very idea of growing and eating sunflower greens (see chapter 8) began with one person, Viktoras Kulvinskas, cofounder of the Hippocrates Health Institute and the author of many books on raw foods, sprouting, and natural living. One scant generation after Viktoras harvested his first crop, most North Americans have heard about sunflower greens, many have eaten them, and some have even grown them. On behalf of sprout growers and microgreen gardeners worldwide, and on my own behalf as one of Viktor's inspired readers and honored friends, I bestow upon him my heartfelt thanks. Thank you, Viktor!

INTRODUCTION

A new world awaits. Are you ready?

For many centuries, our human family has cultivated a wide variety of plants for food. Traditionally, we've grown them to their mature stages in outdoor gardens or on farms. Then, in more recent history, health-conscious eaters everywhere began to grow sprouts from seeds. Nourishing and satisfying, sprouts are easily grown indoors, even in darkness, and require only warm air and fresh rinse water.

Today, growing microgreens indoors is the hot new trend. The young seedlings of vegetables, herbs, beans, and grains, microgreens take a bit more time to grow than sprouts, and unlike sprouts, they require both soil and sunlight. As a result, the tender greens are rich in health-supporting phytonutrients and chlorophyll.

Beyond promising exceptional nutrition, microgreens quench our longing for the freshest possible greens. Dozens of familiar crops can be grown as microgreens, and these varieties delight with diverse colors and flavors. Indeed, microgreens are a feast for both the eyes and the appetite. Possibly the easiest food to prepare, they're best eaten raw and unadorned, but you can also incorporate mild-flavored microgreens into salads and other plant-based dishes. And zesty microgreens, such as radish or mustard greens, can be mixed with more neutral greens or used like a condiment to contribute spice or heat.

If you've mastered the art of growing sprouts—and even if you haven't—it's easy to advance to growing microgreens. You don't need a green thumb to succeed, but you do need patience and persistence. Ultimately, you're likely to discover that tending your microgreen garden will be a joy, not a chore. Be good to your microgreens, and they'll be good for you. One wonderful and free benefit of growing microgreens indoors is that the plants will oxygenate and cleanse the air that you breathe. The room in which you grow microgreens will smell fresh, and even if you become accustomed to this benefit and cease to notice it, visitors to your home surely will.

The following chapters provide in-depth information and detailed instructions that will usher you into an appetizing and nourishing new world. May your future be filled with microgreens, and may all your harvests be bountiful and beautiful!

1

starting your microgreen garden

No matter where you live or what the season, you can be a successful microgreen gardener. By growing microgreens, you gain access to fresh, delectable, organic, and homegrown greens year-round. And all you need to start your indoor garden are seeds, soil, water, and access to a sunny window or grow lights. Chapters 2 through 4 provide all the specifics on these topics.

GO FOR THE GREENS

Microgreens have the potential to be nutritional powerhouses. Although there's very little research on the nutrients they contain, microgreens have been routinely compared to sprouts, which are nutritional giants. Although microgreens may not have quite the vitamin and mineral content of sprouts, they're significant sources of chlorophyll and phytonutrients because they're grown in light, not in darkness as sprouts are.

When exposed to light, a seedling develops chlorophyll. As a nutrient, chlorophyll has antiseptic and anti-inflammatory properties that seem to guard against and even cure some types of anemia.

Phytonutrients are substances in plants (*phyto* means plant) that promote health, prevent disease, and help cure illness, including cancer. These protective nutrients are most concentrated among the large group of plants called *Brassica,* which includes broccoli, cabbage, and kale. Plants produce phytonutrients to protect themselves against environmental stressors and disease—and fortunately for us, when we consume plants, these substances also benefit human health.

WHEN TO HARVEST

Microgreens are very young plants that are generally harvested within four weeks of sowing. Many varieties are ready even earlier; table 1 (page 4) lists ten microgreens that can be harvested after only one week.

1

Microgreens are allowed to grow only long enough to produce one or two sets of leaves. The first leaves are called seed leaves, or cotyledon leaves, and they're the only leaves present during the seed leaf stage. From plant to plant, most seed leaves look identical, especially among the many species of *Brassica*. The second set of leaves takes on more of the characteristics of the mature plant, which is why these leaves are known as true leaves and this stage is called the true leaf stage.

Some microgreens are harvested at the seed leaf stage and others at the true leaf stage based on their flavor, particularly their sweetness. If you were to buy commercially grown microgreens, you'd find that most are cultivated to true leaf stage even if they reach their peak flavor at seed leaf stage. That's because microgreens at true leaf stage are twice the size and weight of those at seed leaf stage, and market competition dictates high-yield harvests. In addition, at seed leaf stage, many microgreens are too fragile to withstand commercial distribution. The advantage of growing your own greens at home is you get to choose when to harvest.

Sample your crops every day and record your impressions so you'll have a record for future use. You'll likely discover that most microgreens taste sweeter and more succulent when grown only to the seed leaf stage, when the leaves contain greater amounts of phytonutrients. If you find a microgreen's taste unappetizing at its seed leaf stage, then grow it to its true leaf stage.

Some microgreens taste better at the true leaf stage because they become milder, as is the case for mustard greens, or less bitter, as is the case for most lettuces. Other crops taste the same at both stages but differ in texture. At the true leaf stage, they become more fibrous and lose the melt-in-your-mouth quality of the seed leaf stage. That's why, if you delay your harvest until after the true leaves have fully developed, your crop will be larger and taller, but it's also likely to be slightly fibrous and bitter. Chapter 5 provides more information about choosing the best time for harvesting.

USING YOUR GREENS

Too often, upscale restaurants relegate microgreens (typically commercially grown and bland) to mere garnishes. Small amounts of greens may even be used to adorn large chunks of meat. I believe microgreens are best eaten raw and just as they are. Dressings are unnecessary, and cooking reduces most microgreens to mush. As with any garden vegetable, it's best to eat microgreens soon after harvest.

In addition, microgreens boast greater amounts of phytonutrients because they're eaten raw. For example, broccoli microgreens are lauded for being fifty times richer in the anticancer phytonutrient sulforaphane than mature broccoli, but in part that's because most people cook mature broccoli before eating it.

If you primarily eat cooked foods, you may find that many varieties of microgreens are an acquired taste. If you favor raw veggies, your palate may adjust more quickly, since microgreens usually taste much the same as raw mature vegetables. For instance, radish microgreens taste like radish tubers; so if you already enjoy raw radishes, you'll savor radish microgreens.

If a specific microgreen doesn't appeal to you initially, keep trying it. Eventually, it just might win you over. While it's true that we eat the foods we crave, the reverse is also true: we learn to crave the foods we eat.

BE VIGILANT

It's important to check your microgreens for mold growth. Mold spores are everywhere, including on seeds and in soil, but the most effective mold deterrent is proper watering. Water microgreens through the soil, not by sprinkling from above; wet microgreens are likely to become moldy microgreens.

This book will suggest ways to use repurposed food containers that fit easily into shallow pools of water so the soil can soak up water from below. Alternatively, you can opt to raise microgreens in cafeteria trays and water them from the side. Chapters 6 and 7 provide instructions for growing microgreens in containers and in trays.

THE TOP TEN MICROGREENS FOR BEGINNERS

For a list of ten excellent choices of microgreens for beginners, see table 1 (page 4). This list takes into account taste, ease of growth, and time to harvest. A significant bonus is that all of the microgreens listed in table 1 germinate in less than three days and can be harvested within one week of sowing.

Other vegetables and herbs, such as carrot, cilantro, dill, and sorrel, are especially delicious as microgreens, but they require a week to germinate and two or more weeks to grow. Even though they're not listed among the top ten microgreens for beginners, these crops are certainly worth trying as you gain experience. Find them listed in table 2 (page 5).

One of the best-tasting microgreens of all is basil, especially the variety deservedly called sweet basil. However, basil requires warm temperatures and its seeds are mucilaginous (sticky when wet), so this crop isn't particularly easy to grow and may present a challenge for some microgreen gardeners. That's why sweet basil appears in table 2 instead of table 1.

TABLE 1. Top ten easiest microgreens for beginners

	MICROGREEN	CHARACTERISTICS	TASTE AND APPEARANCE
1.	Napa cabbage	Grows quickly and easily	Beautiful and flavorful
2.	Radish, red and daikon	Grows quickly and easily	Tastes like the root vegetable
3.	Turnip	Grows quickly and easily	Leaf varieties taste like the root vegetable
4.	Bok choy	Grows quickly and easily	Many different varieties vary in taste and color
5.	Sesame (choose buff or beige seeds, not black)	Germinates rapidly	Tastes better when cooked (a rare exception)
6.	Cress	Grows quickly	Very spicy hot; best eaten sparingly as a condiment
7.	Lettuce, most varieties	Fragile upon harvest	Beautiful and delectable
8.	Asian greens (especially komatsuna)	Tolerates both heat and cold	Has a mild mustard flavor
9.	Endive	Grows easily but slowly	Beautiful bouquet of leaves
10.	Mustard and many mustard greens	Grows quickly and easily	Very spicy hot; best eaten sparingly as a condiment

microgreens to omit

While many plants that are favorites as mature crops can be safely grown as microgreens, I feel a few should be avoided, even though some seed vendors suggest otherwise. Here are eight:

Spinach. Spinach isn't recommended as a microgreen because the seeds' hulls cling tenaciously to the leaves. Since the hulls can't be removed and are inedible, the microgreens are also inedible.

Buckwheat greens. When grown as microgreens and eaten raw, this crop contains dangerous toxins. People shouldn't eat these microgreens, concluded Gilles Arbour, a member of the sprouting and raw-food community, who compiled the well-documented and compelling report, "Are Buckwheat Greens Toxic?," which is available online. While on a health retreat in Florida, Arbour consumed large quantities of buckwheat greens by juicing them. He developed an itching and tingling rash on his suntanned body parts, and he noticed that others at the retreat did too.

TABLE 2.
Ten very delicious but somewhat-challenging-to-grow microgreens

MICROGREEN	CHARACTERISTICS	TASTE AND APPEARANCE
Beet and chard	Difficult to germinate but easy to grow	Beautiful deep color among red varieties
Carrot	Can be very difficult to grow	Subtly sweet
Cilantro	Can be difficult to germinate (even more so than fennel or dill)	Delicious
Fennel and dill	Can be difficult to germinate	Delicious herbal flavors
Pea	Grows rapidly; provides high yields from multiple cuttings; may grow mold	Sweet and succulent when grown in cool temperatures
Red Russian kale	Grows slowly	Sweet and colorful when grown in cold; beautiful at both seed leaf and true leaf stages
Sorrel and marjoram	Grows slowly, leafy	Distinct flavor
Sunflower (choose black oil seeds, not striped)	Has difficulty taking root	Unique flavor
Sweet basil	Grows slowly and fastidiously	Beautiful and delicious
Thai basil	Grows slowly and fastidiously	Second in flavor only to sweet basil

Arbour learned that farmed animals, especially sheep, experience comparable symptoms when they forage on full-grown buckwheat plants. Through chemical analysis of buckwheat greens, he found that a pink-colored toxin called fagopyrin was the origin of his (and the animals') malady.

Unlike the microgreen, raw buckwheat sprouts aren't considered toxic, because soaking and repeated rinsing washes away the toxin, evidenced by the pink tint of the rinse water. Also called kasha, buckwheat groats that are toasted and then boiled aren't implicated either, because cooking neutralizes the toxin.

Canola, chia, and collards. These simply do not taste good.

Celery, corn, and mint. These are very difficult to germinate, germinate very slowly, grow even more slowly, and offer very small yields.

The vast majority of garden seeds won't do for the microgreen gardener. But navigating the seed catalogs won't be intimidating if you know exactly what you're looking for. Keep these guidelines in mind, and you'll have no problems finding the seeds you need and bringing your microgreen garden to life.

THE BENEFITS OF UNTREATED SEED

Seeds that are sown outdoors and allowed to grow into plants during a seasonal cycle are routinely treated with fungicides and sometimes insecticides. The addition of these chemicals poses little health risk to consumers over a long growing season, because the chemicals dissipate over time. However, since seeds that are used for growing microgreens are harvested shortly after germination, when the leaves are extraordinarily young, it's not safe to use treated seeds.

Although there are many kinds of untreated seeds to choose from, they can be a little difficult to track down. While mail-order sources for gardening and farming seeds number in the hundreds, only one or two dozen companies offer the untreated seeds that can be safely used for growing microgreens. (See resources, page 100.)

It should be fairly easy to tell whether a company sells untreated seeds because those that do typically trumpet the fact on catalog covers and website home pages. If you have any doubts, specify that you need untreated seeds when you place your order. When you see packets or product descriptions that don't include the term "untreated," assume that the seeds are treated.

After you find untreated seeds, look for the next important criterion: organic. Whenever possible, purchase organically grown seeds rather than conventionally grown seeds. Bear in mind that while all organic seeds are untreated, not all untreated seeds are organic.

Organic seeds are less likely to harbor pathogens, such as *E. coli* or salmonella, that lead to food-borne illness, especially in uncooked foods. These pathogens have their origins in animal agriculture, and they can survive in soil that has been fertilized by manure that has not been fully composted. Seeds that are harvested from this soil can be contaminated. It also pays to grow your microgreens in organic soil that's free of animal-based fertilizers (see chapter 3).

CHOOSING QUALITY SEEDS

When it comes to growing microgreens, ordering seeds from garden seed companies (rather than sprout seed sources) is a good idea. The best garden seed companies provide ample information about their seeds on packets and in product descriptions. Since these companies make the effort to compile and provide helpful information, their seeds may cost a little more, but the extra expense is worth it.

The following pointers are what to look for when reading a seed packet or catalog description. If the criteria below are met, then you've found a winning source for your microgreen seeds.

CULTIVAR NAME. Specific varieties of a single species of a cultivated plant are called cultivars. Dozens and sometimes hundreds of cultivars have been selectively bred for each species of food plant. For example, there are many cultivars of Italian broccoli, a commonly grown microgreen that Westerners know simply as "broccoli." (Italian broccoli differs from Romanesco broccoli, Chinese broccoli, broccoli rabe, and broccoflower, which are all distinctly different species.)

When a label includes the cultivar name, you're able to identify the specific variety of plant. When you find a favorite, you can seek it out consistently over time by looking for the cultivar name on seed packets or in catalogs.

cultivating variety

Although broccoli is a valuable case study in terms of the number of cultivars that may be available within a species, untreated broccoli seeds that are sold specifically for growing sprouts or microgreens are rarely identified by cultivar. Instead, they're labeled simply and generically as "broccoli" and always cost less than broccoli seeds whose cultivars are named. Even microgreen broccoli seeds purchased from the same source at different times may not share the same cultivar. This may not matter, as you might not taste any difference among cultivars of broccoli when they're grown only to the microgreen stage. However, over time you may find that specific cultivars of certain species become your favorites, so keeping notes of the names of the cultivars you prefer can pay off.

DATE OF HARVEST. The date of harvest is important because you can use it to forecast seed longevity. Some companies print the date of packaging or an expiration date on seed packets, neither of which is the same, or as helpful to you, as the harvest date. In general, use seeds within five years of harvest; if you don't know the harvest date, plan to use the seeds within five years of purchase.

GERMINATION RATE. In any batch of seeds, a certain number can be predicted not to germinate, and companies describe the germination rate on seed packets as a percentage. Any seed that has a germination rate lower than 90 percent is unsuitable for microgreen gardening since the errant 10 percent will rot. Because seeds are sown closely together in microgreen gardening, the faulty seeds are likely to cause nearby seeds to rot too, threatening the entire harvest.

ORGANIC CERTIFICATION. For seed vendors located in the United States, organic certification need not necessarily mean US Department of Agriculture (USDA) certification. Regional certifying agencies also monitor and attest to organic farming methods, but they're not permitted to use the words "organically grown" on seed packets. Other terminology, such as "naturally grown," may be used, and that's perfectly acceptable.

BOTANICAL NAMES. Scientific names are given in Latin or sometimes Greek and are recognizable because they're italicized. Determining the botanical names of the seeds you purchase is the best way to be sure of what you're getting. It's especially useful to know the botanical names of foreign plant species. For example, the botanical name for bok choy, also known as pak choi, is *Brassica chinensis*. Even English plant names can cause confusion if a US seed catalog uses the British name for a plant that's also commonly grown in the United States. For example, the terms "cos" and "rocket" are the British names for romaine and arugula. When the scientific name is given, there can be no confusion about such foreign terms.

BUYING IN BULK

Buying small packets of seeds is ideal if you're experimenting with growing microgreens or figuring out which microgreens you like best. When you're ready to set up an ongoing growing operation and you've identified the seeds you prefer, consider reordering a quantity in bulk.

Seed prices vary widely from species to species and among cultivars within a species; some are very inexpensive, while others are extravagantly priced.

Buying in bulk can ease the cost burden. So even if you're only interested in buying seed packets now, think about buying from a seed supplier that also sells in bulk. This option may be important to you in the future.

While seed packets contain a specific number of seeds, bulk seeds are sold by weight. They're available by the ounce (twenty-five grams), one-quarter pound (one hundred grams), or pound (one-half kilo). If you find seeds that you like in small packets, reorder in bulk as early as possible to ensure you're getting seeds from the same crop.

PAMPER YOUR SEEDS

Seeds are highly perishable, and untreated seeds in particular must be pampered. If only a fraction of the seeds you plant won't germinate due to poor storage conditions, you may develop a serious mold problem that can spread throughout your crop. To grow successfully, your seeds need to maintain viability (the seeds' ability to germinate) and vigor (a measure of the seeds' strength and health). Vigor declines before viability, so even if a batch of seeds successfully germinates, the seedlings may not grow vigorously.

The best conditions for storing seeds are in airtight containers in a cold place with even temperatures (above freezing) and low humidity—such as a refrigerator. Other good alternatives include a wine cellar, root cellar, or other cold storage. Before refrigerating seeds, first remove them from seed packets, envelopes, or other packaging and transfer them to glass jars, preferably jars that have gaskets inside the lids. Check to see that the gasket is pliable so that the lid will seal tightly; with age, gaskets can turn brittle and no longer create an airtight seal.

Ordinarily, storing seeds in plastic bags isn't ideal because bags are watertight but not airtight. However, a new generation of vacuum-sealed plastic packaging (one brand name is Cryovac) effectively seals out air and moisture and creates an airtight seal. The packaging works with vacuum food sealing machines designed for home use, and it could rival glass jars when it comes to effectively storing and protecting seeds. To verify that a vacuum-sealed plastic package is airtight, check to see whether you can smell the contents through a sealed bag. If any odor can be detected, air is seeping in.

Whether you use jars or vacuum-sealed bags to store seeds, the final important step is to label each container with details about the seeds inside. At the minimum, include the name of the seed, its source, and the date of harvest or purchase. An excellent and convenient method for making sure you have all of the pertinent information about the seed you're storing is to trim the original label from the envelope or bag and tape it to the storage container.

Even when seeds are properly stored, their vigor will eventually diminish until they're no longer worth sowing. Longevity varies among species, but storing seeds longer than five years isn't recommended. So if you're buying in bulk, purchase no more seed than you can store in your refrigerator and use within five years.

SOAKING SEEDS

If you'd like to accelerate the germination process, you have the option of soaking seeds, usually for eight to twelve hours, before planting. Soaking is recommended not only for faster germination, which can decrease total growing time by as much as one day, but also to soften the pods and hulls. It may be easier for emerging leaves to shuck off the softened pods and hulls of seeds that have been soaked. However, not all seeds should be soaked. (See sidebar, below.)

To soak seeds before sowing, fill a small jar with water and seeds, screw on the lid, and shake. Shaking aerates the water, which aids germination. While the seeds are soaking, remove the lid from the jar so that air can flow freely. When the seeds are ready for sowing, drain off the water using a sieve or sprouting jar lid with a built-in strainer.

to soak or not to soak

Soaking seeds, although optional, can hasten germination and loosen pods and hulls. Here are general guidelines for deciding which seeds to soak before planting.

The following seeds *may be* soaked before sowing:

- medium seeds with husks (such as dill and fennel)
- large seeds (such as peas and wheat)
- large seeds in hard shells (such as cilantro and sunflower)
- seeds in hard pods (such as beet and chard)

The following seeds *should not* be soaked before sowing:

- tiny seeds (such as lettuce seeds)
- mucilaginous seeds, or seeds that when moistened are sticky or secrete a sticky substance (such as arugula, basil, or flax)

Seeds that have been soaked should be covered with soil when they're planted. When you cover soaked seeds with soil, their pods and hulls stay thoroughly moistened and will be naturally cast off as the seedlings push up through the soil. Otherwise, you'll need to remove many of the pods and hulls manually when it's time to harvest. One exception to this rule is sunflower seeds; for unknown reasons, covering sunflower seeds with soil seems to cement the hull to the leaf.

TECHNIQUES FOR SOWING

The most common mistake that beginners (and even some veterans) make when planting microgreens is to sow the seeds too close together. This can result in overly thick growth, which traps moisture among the stems and fosters mold growth that can ruin the entire harvest. So always err on the side of sowing the seeds too thinly. Don't allow seeds to overlap or have contact with other seeds.

With practice, you'll get the knack for using the optimal number of seeds and controlling the distribution so it's even. Try using deep-bowled measuring spoons not only for measuring seeds but also for sowing them. Hold the spoon with your thumb and middle finger and gently tap the handle with your forefinger to drop the seed. Tapping the spoon, rather than shaking it, gives you more precise control. The seeds will drop only from the side of the spoon that faces you. An alternative method for sowing small seeds is to fill an emptied salt or pepper shaker and shake the seeds out of the shaker. (For tips on how to premeasure the right amount of seeds for sowing, see page 40.)

On the day of planting and until the seeds germinate, closely examine the soil to see if there are any gaps between seeds. Some tiny seeds, notably basils and many lettuces, are the same dark brownish-black color as the soil, so at first it's difficult to see where you've planted. Within minutes of contact with moist soil, however, basil seeds swell and turn purple.

to cover or not to cover

When planting your microgreen garden, cover only seeds that have been soaked (except sunflower seeds, which are the exception to this rule). When planting all other seeds, gently press the seeds into the soil, but *do not* cover them with soil.

Soon enough, bare spots in the soil will be apparent, and you can add seeds where needed. For other seeds, you may have to wait until they begin to germinate. The radicle, or root, that first sprouts is usually light in color and easily visible. You can still fill in the gaps during this early germination stage; the latecomer seeds will lag behind by only one or two days.

For all *except* mucilaginous seeds and soaked seeds, use your finger to gently press the seeds into the soil. *Do not* cover the seeds with soil. If you do, when the succulent leaves emerge, many will be encrusted with earth.

the inside scoop: seeds

- Buy untreated seeds from a dependable source. (See resources, page 100.)
- Ideally, choose certified organic seeds or seeds that are labeled "naturally grown."
- At first, purchase small packets of seeds. As you gain experience growing different crops, buy your favorite seeds in bulk for the best value.
- Choose only a limited number of varieties to start. (See table 1, page 4.)
- Store seeds in airtight glass jars in the refrigerator and use them within five years of their harvest date, if known, or purchase date.
- Consider soaking certain seeds before planting for faster germination.
- Cover only soaked seeds with soil when planting. For all others, use your finger to gently press the seeds into the soil, ensuring contact but not covering the seeds.

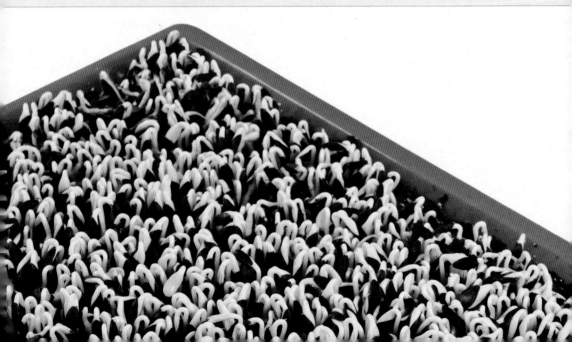

sowing and watering

Just as choosing the right seeds is critical to the success of your microgreen garden, there are different growing mediums you can consider. In addition, water quality can affect not only how microgreens grow but also how they taste. Ultimately, what you learn about soil and water will help you strike a balance by providing sufficient moisture without promoting the growth of mold and rot, the greatest threats to microgreens.

GET THE DIRT ON SOIL

If you've ever grown sprouts, you know that air and water will do the job—no soil required. That's not the case for microgreens, which grow best in soil. You can use commercial potting soil, seedling mix (also called seed-starting mix and grow mix), or a combination of the two. These are the recommended growing mediums whether you decide to grow your microgreens in containers or in trays.

As good as topsoil is for outdoor crops, it's not the ideal choice for growing microgreens. The soil used in microgreen gardening is dispensed into small containers or spread thinly in trays. If you do this with topsoil, it will compact and harden, blocking air and suffocating the microgreen roots. This problem can be avoided by using commercial mixes that contain soil additives, such as perlite or vermiculite (which granulate and break up the soil) and peat moss or milled sphagnum peat (which make the soil light and spongy).

In commercial mixes, peat serves an additional purpose: it's a natural fungicide. Fungi spores can be found everywhere, and fungi can grow on seeds or on emerging roots and stems. A broad range of fungal diseases (collectively called "damping-off") can cause seedlings to rot at the soil line and die. Topsoil from an outdoor garden is likely to be full of spores, but commercial mixes that contain peat offer more protection. Just as troubling, the same topsoil may harbor pests or introduce weeds and microorganisms not only to your microgreens but also to your home. To decrease the risk of contamination, commercial potting soils or seedling mixes are pasteurized or sterilized. (If you decide to try growing microgreens using soil from your own yard or garden, sterilize it by baking it in the oven at 212 degrees F for at least 30 minutes.)

Pick Your Mix

You can customize the growing mix to conform to a specific plant's growing cycle. For example, crops that have a short growth cycle (ten or fewer days from planting to harvest) can grow exclusively in seedling mix. Microgreen roots are able to gain anchorage more easily in seedling mixes than in potting soils, and seedling mixes have sufficient nutrients to sustain plants for almost two weeks. (See table 1, page 4, for a list of ten microgreen crops that can be harvested within one week of sowing; these are ideal for growing in seedling mix.)

Microgreen crops that have a medium growth cycle (two to three weeks) do well in potting soil. Another option is to fill the bottom half of a container or tray with potting soil and the top half with seedling mix. The seeds will germinate and take root in the seedling mix. As the roots reach deeper, they'll find the potting soil and the nutritious boost it provides. In this way, using half potting soil and half seedling mix can offer the best of both worlds.

For microgreens that have a long growth cycle (four weeks or more), potting soil with added fertilizer is recommended. Typically, microgreens don't need fertilizer because they grow so quickly, but longer-growing plants may need the extra nutrition. (For more information about fertilizers, see "Boost Those Roots with Caution," page 15.)

Seedling mix and potting soil are most economical when purchased in large quantities, so buy the largest bags that you can comfortably lift. Of course, just as you might want to start out with small packets of seeds until you find your favorites, you may want to purchase smaller bags of growing medium and experiment until you discover what works best for you.

Table 3 (page 15) provides a timetable that can help you determine when to use seedling mix, potting soil, and fertilizer. Keep in mind that these general recommendations are based on how long the different growing mediums are likely to remain fertile. How quickly the soil will be depleted depends on many factors, such as the type of seed you're using, the amount of soil you're using, and how densely the seeds are sown.

Dig Deeper (Even If the Label States "Organic")

As discussed in chapter 2, buying untreated seeds is essential and choosing organic seeds is encouraged. Similarly, using organic potting soil and seedling mixes can enhance microgreen growth and protect you from potential

TABLE 3. Soil use as determined by the plant's growth cycle

TIME FROM PLANTING TO HARVEST	LEAF STAGE AT HARVEST	TYPE OF SOIL
5 to 10 days	seed leaf stage	seedling mix
10 days to 2 weeks	seed leaf or early true leaf stage	seedling mix may suffice, but potting soil is recommended
2 to 3 weeks	true leaf stage	potting soil or a combination (half potting soil on the bottom and half seedling mix on the top)
4 weeks or more	true leaf stage	potting soil with added fertilizer

exposure to harmful pathogens. So be on the lookout for soil mixes that are labeled organic, but be warned that you'll need to read the fine print to learn the true contents of even organic growing mediums.

Organic mixes can contain ingredients that originate in factory farms and slaughterhouses, the modern breeding grounds for microbes that endanger the world's food supply. Still, the USDA permits the "organic" label on soil mixes that contain urea (urine), manure (feces), blood meal, and bone meal that have their source in industrial animal agriculture. Other common additives—such as feather meal and poultry litter (a mixture of chicken or turkey excreta, spilled feed, feathers, and bedding materials)—originate from the most diseased of all factory-farmed animals. These additives are laced with pesticides that were once fed to the chickens and turkeys (even the feces of these animals won't attract insects), yet composted poultry manure is decreed organic by the USDA.

Boost Those Roots with Caution

Fertilizer use is optional, almost always unnecessary, and may even be detrimental in microgreen gardening. Microgreens that are grown in soil typically don't need much fertilizer of any kind; the small amount of nutrients in the soil is sufficient for sustaining the tender plants through their relatively short growing cycles. However, as outlined in table 3, longer-growing crops may benefit from the addition of fertilizer. And fertilizer is absolutely necessary when microgreens are grown hydroponically, or without soil, which is a practice that shows potential. (See sidebar, page 16.)

For those who decide to use fertilizer when growing microgreens, watersoluble liquid fertilizers can yield the most immediate results. Liquid kelp extract is among the best fertilizers and is probably one of the least expensive. However, using too great a concentration of kelp can inhibit germination, which is why liquid kelp is generally marketed as a foliar spray intended for application to the undersides of leaves. This technique isn't appropriate for microgreen gardening, though. If you decide to use liquid kelp, add it to the soil before planting and do so very sparingly. The time to add the fertilizer is when you saturate the soil. (See "Preparing the Soil," opposite page.)

Solid fertilizers—such as compost, humus, powdered kelp, pulverized minerals, or ground shells—aren't useful in microgreen gardening. That's because, like time-release pills, they simply don't have enough time to relinquish their helpful contents during the typical one or two weeks of seedling growth. What's more, these fertilizers accelerate microgreen growth only slightly, if at all. At most, the potential benefit might be shaving off one day of growing time, which could be profitable for professional microgreen farmers but is inconsequential for home gardeners.

the alternative to soil: hydroponics

Hydroponics involves raising plants in nutrient solutions instead of soil. Plant roots that are bathed in diluted liquid fertilizers latch on to a growing medium, such as cloth made of natural fibers like coir (the fuzzy lining inside coconut shells) or burlap (which is made from jute). In place of coir or burlap, other mediums, such as plates and bowls made of woven bamboo or straw, can be used. Other natural growing mediums include rock wool, volcanic cinder, crushed granite, and inland sand, but all of these can be messy. One effective synthetic medium is foam pads woven from polyethylene, the plastic from which most food containers are made. In fact, the practice of using polyethylene foam pads in conjunction with liquid fertilizers has proved very successful for growing microgreens, although the pads tend to promote mold growth.

Adaptations of the basic hydroponics technique include aeroponics (constant misting), bioponics (underwater aquaponics for plants), and vermiponics (systems using compost tea and worm castings). Hydroponics and all of these other soil-free growing methods have a considerable downside, though. All require costly start-up, a bulky setup, and the willingness to use man-made products, including stews of supplemental fertilizers that are seldom organic. Even water-soluble organic fertilizers are usually made up of composted urine, feces, and blood from factory-farmed animals, and these fertilizers aren't likely to appeal to microgreen gardeners who make dietary choices for reasons of health, ethics, or the environment.

Eliminating undesirable fertilizers is unlikely to lead to success in hydroponics or other soil-free growing methods. When microgreens are grown without fertilizers upon coir, burlap, bamboo, straw, or polyethylene, the plants develop unusually slowly and become stunted or dwarfed. Even those that look nearly normal taste either bitter or bland. So, in the absence of soil, liquid fertilizer is indeed required.

Preparing the Soil

Before you layer the potting soil or seedling mix in a container or tray, an essential first step is to put the soil in a clean bucket and stir in water. The goal is to use enough water to saturate the soil but not to use so much that the water puddles on top of the soil or in the bottom of the bucket. As you stir the water into the soil, remove any leaves, twigs, wood chips, or other fibers that may be in the soil. If you wait to add water to the soil until it's already in the container or tray, it will be much harder to stir the soil and remove unwanted debris, and too easy to spill water onto your table or floor.

Ideally, reserve one bucket that will be used exclusively for this step in microgreen gardening. At the minimum, use a bucket that harbors no remnants of chemical cleaners or other undesirable substances. Between batches of soil, allow the empty bucket to dry out and remain dry for at least one day as a safeguard against mold. Remember, damp soil may promote plant growth, but it will also foster the growth of mold.

WATER QUALITY

Water can have a surprising effect on microgreens. It's essential for the plant's growth, of course, but these tender indoor plants grow for only a short time, and for that reason, the palatability and the quality of the water can actually be reflected in the *taste* of the microgreens.

There are simple ways to evaluate the quality of your water. If the taste dissuades you from drinking the water, then don't use it on your microgreens. Sprouts, which must be bathed in water several times daily, are similarly affected by water quality. If you successfully grow sprouts, then your water is probably fine for growing microgreens.

Another easy and conclusive experiment is to compare the growth and taste of microgreens that are hydrated with different water sources. Grow two batches of the same seeds in the same soil and under identical conditions of light, darkness, and warmth, but use water from different sources. For example, hydrate one batch with water from the faucet and the other with bottled spring water. After two weeks, make an assessment. Do the two batches of microgreens look the same? Do they taste the same? After all, the quality of the water you use is best judged by the quality of the microgreens the water produces.

The two factors that are most likely to influence water quality are chlorine and pH levels. Chlorine is the predominate additive in municipal tap water that affects microgreens, and the pH of a solution refers to how alkaline or acidic it is.

CHLORINATED WATER. In your test case, chlorine is the likely culprit if the greens that are hydrated with tap water become slightly yellow or curled but the other batch does not. While chlorine has long been added to tap water to kill bacteria, levels now far exceed those of past decades.

To remove chlorine from tap water, fill a wide-mouthed container, such as a bucket, with chlorinated tap water and allow it to sit uncovered for twenty-four hours. The chlorine will evaporate. Alternatively, use an activated charcoal filter to trap and remove chlorine from tap water. Filters are very convenient since they remove chlorine immediately. However, compared to a bucket, which is cheap and can be used again and again, filters are costly and must be replaced.

WATER PH. Microgreens do best when grown with slightly acidic water in the narrow pH range between 6 and 6.5, which is close to neutral. Alkaline water (above 7 pH) could be to blame if your seeds routinely show slow or poor germination regardless of the ambient temperature or if your seedlings tend to rot even with frugal watering.

If you want to know the pH level of your tap water or any other water that you use to grow microgreens, you can buy a pH kit from a gardening store. Two types of pH tests are sold for testing water. The most convenient option includes strips of litmus paper that can be dipped into the water; the other option includes vials of liquid that can be mixed with the water.

If your tap water scores above 7, there's a simple household remedy that can be used to lower its pH. Try adding a small amount of lemon juice to make the water more acidic. Start with less than one-quarter teaspoon of lemon juice per gallon of water, then test again. If needed, add another one-quarter teaspoon of lemon juice and retest. While lemon juice is preferred, vinegar can also do the trick.

This discussion about pH may make you wonder not only about the pH of your water but also of your soil, but don't be concerned. Commercial potting soils and seedling mixes already have the appropriate pH balance.

Forget the Watering Can

There's no question that the water used to hydrate your microgreens is important, and it's equally true that *how* you water your microgreen garden—and *how much* you water it—makes a world of difference. The methods that you use to keep the soil and seeds moist (but not too moist) are your weapons against rot and mold.

A common error in microgreen gardening is to water the young plants from above, which is called top watering. Because microgreens are so densely packed, the canopy of leaves and the stems catch and hold water if it comes from above, which prevents the water from reaching the soil. The water will stagnate on the leaves and stems, causing mold to grow and the stems to rot. The alternatives to top watering are bottom watering and side watering. Both methods introduce water directly to the soil rather than to the plants.

BOTTOM WATERING. The best way to hydrate microgreens that are grown in containers is from the bottom; all you have to do is put the containers in a shallow pool of water and let the soil soak up the water from below. More information about bottom watering can be found in the chapter about container gardening (chapter 6).

SIDE WATERING. The preferred method for watering microgreens that are grown in trays is side watering. This simply requires pouring the water onto the soil from the sides of the trays and allowing the excess to drain off. More information about side watering can be found in the chapter about tray gardening (chapter 7).

Spray and Cover

Although it's essential to avoid top watering after the seedlings begin to grow, it's safe to spray the seeds from above to keep them moist before germination. In fact, spraying the seeds is essential. That's because unsoaked microgreen seeds aren't buried in the soil, so they dry out quickly.

SPRAY THE SEEDS. To moisten the seeds, avoid using the kitchen sink's pull-out spray hose, which is likely to create a torrential downpour that dislodges the seeds and allows unwanted puddles to form. Instead, try using a spray bottle or fine mister to spritz the seeds; spray bottles are much easier to adjust than sink spray hoses. You can even repurpose a spray container from a non-toxic household cleaner. To fully rinse away any residue, fill the container with hot water, allow the water to sit in the container until it cools, and pour out the water. If you repeat this process twice, the residue should be gone; to make sure, smell and taste the spray to confirm that the water is untainted.

As always, take precautions with your equipment to prevent the growth of bacteria and mold. Between crops, dismantle the spray bottle and remove the sprayer from its container. Stand the sprayer upside down and allow both the sprayer and the empty bottle to dry out completely.

COVER THE SEEDS. After you've sprayed the seeds, put a damp cotton cloth over them to discourage evaporation and retain moisture. Choose undyed cotton cloth that's thin, smooth, and has a wide weave, such as the fabric from a bed sheet; avoid heavy fabrics, such as terrycloth or cotton bath towels. Cut a piece of fabric so that it has the same dimensions as the container or tray. Put the dry cloth on top of the seeds, then spray the cloth with water. For subsequent sprayings, it's possible to leave the cloth where it is and simply spray the seeds directly through the cloth. The danger in not removing the cloth is that you can oversaturate the soil but not know it. Covered seeds typically need to be sprayed once each day.

Here are a couple of other precautions. While cloth is recommended, paper towels can also be used. However, they're not as suitable as cloth because soaked seeds are much more likely to cling to paper towels than to cloth. In addition, not all seeds should be covered. Don't use cloth when starting mucilaginous seeds, such as arugula, basil, cress, and flax, because these sticky seeds will cling to the cloth rather than to the soil.

For your first several crops, you may prefer to skip using the cloth so you can view the unfolding miracle of germination. This is understandable. Feel free to postpone using the cloth or simply dispense with it altogether. Providing a top lid to your container both helps to retain moisture and provides a clear view of the germination that is unfolding, so rather than using cloth, use the lid. (For more information, see the section on preparing containers on page 38.) If you use neither, be sure to check the seeds two or three times each day and spritz them with water if they look dry.

the inside scoop: soil and water

- Grow microgreens in commercial soil mixes, such as potting soil, seedling mix, or a combination of the two.
- Choose organic soil mixes if possible, but be aware that even organic mixes can contain undesirable contents, including animal urine, feces, blood meal, and bone meal. Read labels carefully.
- In general, avoid using fertilizer when growing microgreens in soil.
- Before putting the soil in containers or trays, put it in a bucket and stir in enough water to saturate the soil.
- Be particular about the water you use to hydrate microgreens. Taste and test the water to make sure it isn't overly chlorinated and doesn't have an undesirable pH level.
- To prevent mold growth and rot, avoid watering microgreens from the top. Use the bottom-watering method when growing microgreens in containers and the side-watering method when growing microgreens in trays.
- Before seeds germinate, spritz them with water at least once each day and keep them covered to retain moisture.

4

promoting germination and growth

Generally, germination requires warmth, water, and oxygen. Once germinated, all microgreens need is light. By using a number of techniques and tools, you can simulate the sun's warmth and light so you can grow microgreens indoors all year round. Factors that encourage growth outdoors, such as wind and fresh air, also benefit your indoor microgreen garden and can be simulated, just like warmth and light.

HEAT THINGS UP

Warmth and Germination

Most seeds will germinate at room temperature, which is around 70 degrees F (21 degrees C) during the day and somewhat lower during the night. There are, of course, exceptions to this rule; some seeds, such as celery, most lettuces, and pea, don't need as much warmth to germinate. At either extreme, most seeds used to grow microgreens will germinate at temperatures between 50 degrees F (10 degrees C) and 85 degrees F (29 degrees C). Even indoors, summers can be too hot and winters too cold.

If you live in a cold climate and keep your home cool during the winter, you can encourage seeds to germinate by positioning microgreen containers or trays near a radiator or heater or on top of a seedling heat mat. Because it's designed specifically for this purpose, the mat's low wattage won't melt plastic containers. Note, however, that seedling heat mats should be used with caution if you're growing microgreens in seedling pots or repurposed plastic food containers, both of which are made of polyethylene (recycling number 1). Exposure to heat can cause chemicals in this type of plastic to migrate into the soil. That's why these plastic containers *should not* be put in direct contact with heat mats even if the mat manufacturer claims that use with plastics is safe.

If your kitchen cabinets are made of metal, you're in luck. By affixing seedling heat mats to a metal cabinet's inner walls, you can create an

germination on the fast track

Germination times vary widely from species to species, but for seeds commonly regarded as suitable for microgreens, you can count on less than one week. Often you can discount the germination times listed on the seed packet, because these times are based on outdoor planting. For instance, if "one to two weeks" is stated, don't be surprised if your seeds germinate in only one to two days. Similarly, if a two- to three-week germination time is given, you might see delicate seedlings emerge in only two to three days. This is because microgreen seeds aren't buried in soil; they have more access to warmth and light. Also, seeds that are sown indoors are exposed to more consistent warmth than those that are sown outdoors.

indoor germination space that's ideal for starting microgreens or growing sprouts. Lacking a metal cabinet, you can construct a germination terrarium by adhering heat mats to the walls of an empty glass aquarium with an aluminum top. If you shop for a fish tank at a pet supply store, you can purchase reptile heat mats as an alternative to seedling heat mats, since both types of mats output the same low wattage. Reptile heat mats may be more convenient because they already have adhesive on the bottom, making them perfect for affixing to the walls of metal cabinets or glass aquariums.

The heated cabinets or aquariums can be used to boost germination from fall through spring. They're especially effective in the winter; even when the nighttime kitchen temperature descends to 60 degrees F (15.5 degrees C) or lower, the cabinet or aquarium interior remains at 70 degrees F (21 degrees C) or higher.

Warmth and Growth

Once germinated, most seedlings can tolerate fluctuations from 60 to 80 degrees F (15.5 to 27 degrees C). Dill, lettuce, onion, pea, and most *Brassicas* actually flourish at 60 degrees F (15.5 degrees C) and are ideal winter crops. Cooler temperatures can even enhance the pigmentation of *Brassicas*; for example, red bok choy's leaves grow rosy and purple turnip's stems stain a royal hue only with exposure to relative cold.

On the other hand, cooler temperatures can slow down many species of microgreens that aren't *Brassicas*, such as beet, carrot, celery, many herbs, some lettuces, and sunflower. These microgreens can be harvested after only one week's growth in summer and can take up to two weeks to mature during the colder days and shorter daylight hours of winter. And at 60 to 65 degrees F (15.5 to 18 degrees C), certain microgreens, such as basil, dig in their heels and refuse to budge an inch. These you can simply postpone growing until spring.

REGULATING LIGHT

Light and Germination

While warmth is instrumental in germination, light is much less important (which is why you can successfully germinate microgreens even in a metal cabinet). Indoors, most seeds used for growing microgreens aren't fussy and will germinate equally well in either daylight or darkness. Outdoor gardeners sow seeds beneath a layer of soil to protect them from burning sun, blowing wind, and pecking birds—the darkness underground typically doesn't affect germination. And while different seeds have different needs, they all share one trait: once germinated, all plants, including microgreens, need light.

Light and Growth

The sun's light is the gold standard, and direct sunlight fosters the most succulent plant growth. For the best results, microgreens should be exposed to

TABLE 4. Microgreens that grow well in indirect sunlight

BRASSICAS	HERBS	OTHER
Arugula	Chervil	Amaranth
Some bok choys (partial shade)	Cilantro (during first week)	Lettuces (many varieties)
Most mustard greens	Dill	
Tatsoi		

at least ten hours of light and at least six hours of darkness each day. Under weak or scant sunlight, microgreens will need more days to grow, but they'll still grow; if necessary, indirect sunlight sometimes can suffice as long as the seedlings rest on the window sill. In fact, some seedlings flourish only in indirect sunlight. (See table 4, above.)

The terms "direct light," "direct sunlight," and "full sun" are synonymous terms. "Indirect light," "indirect sunlight," and "shade" also describe the same conditions. However, don't confuse *indirect* light with *insufficient* light. Indirect sunlight from alongside a window can provide sufficient light for some microgreens, but insufficient light promotes the wrong kind of growth. Seedlings in search of light grow tall (which is undesirable in microgreens). They also lack strength and vigor and don't develop the deep green color that signals they're rich in chlorophyll, the marker of healthy microgreens.

When they're exposed to sufficient sunlight, microgreens grow not so much tall as wide, which is desirable. Under insufficient light, seedlings grow long, frail stems in a fruitless attempt to reach for more light. Gardeners call this sad state "legginess," and you want to avoid it at all costs because leggy greens tend to be tough and bitter.

Some microgreen gardeners attempt to remedy legginess by keeping seedlings in darkness for one or two days after germination. This technique involves covering the microgreens with a plate or other weight. Weighed down, the seedlings grow stems that are strong and squat, but they also tend to become fibrous and bitter too.

Chlorophyll in the leaves converts light energy into sugars, starches, and other rich nutrients. It also imparts the deep color in dark leafy green vegetables such as collards and kale. The darker and richer the green in a plant's leaf, the more chlorophyll it has, and more chlorophyll means the plant can produce greater amounts of other phytonutrients and sugars. More sugars result in more flavorful vegetables.

USING SUNLIGHT

A popular method for accessing light is to grow microgreens indoors in front of a window. Though glass filters out most of the ultraviolet spectrum of light, microgreens can flourish without a full spectrum. A single-paned window can be used when it creates a hothouse effect and temperatures don't get too high. But if the sunlight shines through the glass into a small, confined space with poor ventilation, microgreens can bake in hot weather.

If just one of your windows provides direct sunlight for at least half of the day, you'll have enough light for growing microgreens. If the windowsill is too small to hold your containers or trays of microgreens, consider constructing shelves in front of the window. This can be done affordably using materials such as pinewood shelves and basic metal brackets. If you construct shelves across a window, you may be surprised and disappointed by how much light the shelves themselves block out. You can compensate immensely by painting the shelves a high-gloss white, which reflects much light. Even if you have to build shelves in front of a window, the material costs will be offset if you can avoid artificial lighting, which requires electricity.

USING ARTIFICIAL LIGHT

While natural sunlight is desirable for growing microgreens, the amount of light available will be dictated by where you live and the time of year. A sensible method for augmenting natural light is to use electric indoor lighting. Resort to artificial lighting as a supplement to, not a substitute for, natural sunlight. With this approach, you'll only need to use artificial light for part of the year, and then for only part of the day. Compared to summer light, winter light not only lasts fewer hours, but it's also weaker. So you might need to extend daylight hours with artificial lighting only during the winter; think of the electric lights as providing transitional twilight rather than noontime sun.

Just as you would if growing the plants entirely in natural daylight, plan to expose microgreens to ten hours or more of combined natural and artificial light. Long hours of natural light do reach a natural limit, which is a good thing. Artificial light can exceed that limit, and this isn't desirable. Unlimited light doesn't necessarily produce unlimited growth; plants need a minimum of six hours of darkness. During that time they metabolize and convert carbohydrates into plant tissue, deepen their roots, thicken their stems, and broaden their leaves.

In an effort to maximize yields, some growers shine electric lights twenty-four hours a day for the last two to three days before harvest. With uninterrupted light and no darkness, microgreens continue to create starches and sugars but only minimally metabolize them, leading to a greater *quantity* of growth but not a greater *quality* of growth. Even if it's not visibly apparent after only two or three days of around-the-clock light, plants become stressed.

Microgreens that are grown under artificial lights around the clock can't provide us with the same level of nutrients as those grown under conditions that closely resemble what occurs in nature. This is reflected in the taste of the plants: there's a sharp contrast between the bland, bitter flavor of microgreens grown under perpetual light and the intense, sweet flavor of microgreens that are grown in light alternating with darkness.

Flip the Switch

Because they typically grow for only one or two weeks, microgreens grow equally well when nurtured with standard cool white fluorescent lamps or full-spectrum grow lights. If you already own standard fluorescents (perhaps you're using this type of bulb to illuminate this very page), go ahead and use what you have for growing microgreens. If it hovers closely over your greens, a single fluorescent tube can suffice, but two would be better. Fluo-

enhance light with simple reflectors

Reflectors can intensify either natural sunlight or artificial light. You don't need cumbersome mirrors to make reflectors; lightweight white cardboard works beautifully. Because the undersides of produce boxes are usually white, your local grocer could be a convenient and inexpensive source. A deluxe reflector can be made from white foam core board, which consists of two poster boards with a foam core center. Look for foam core board in office and art supply stores. Coating cardboard is also an option: aluminum foil is more reflective than white foam core, but you may find it more unsightly. The high-tech version of foil is metalized Mylar, a plastic film covered with aluminum. Some very large and well-stocked gardening stores carry metalized Mylar, as do the very smallest sporting goods stores, where Mylar is sold as space blankets or survival blankets.

To make a reflector, trim the boards to the preferred size, cover with foil or Mylar if using either, and prop the boards upright around the microgreens. To make the boards stand upright, create a fold that you can anchor under the tray of microgreens; simply make one fold two or three inches (5 to 7.5 centimeters) from the edge of the board and slide the folded edge under the tray. This creates a lightweight light box that's collapsible when not in use and easy to store. If your light source is natural sunlight, using only one board works wonders.

rescents flicker constantly, although they do so too quickly for the human eye to notice. That's why fluorescent fixtures usually house double tubes, so that each tube compensates for the other.

Full-spectrum bulbs are necessary if you're growing flowering or fruiting plants, but microgreens never reach these stages. Still, full-spectrum bulbs can be effective when growing microgreens. Again, use what you have. If you already own full-spectrum bulbs, put them to use as grow lights.

Supplemental lighting for growing microgreens doesn't need to be complicated or expensive. In some costly setups, the light units are suspended on chains so the lights can be adjusted to hover closely above the plants as they grow. Such an elaborate arrangement is unnecessary; instead, you can control the distance between the lights and the plants simply by propping the containers or trays atop varying sizes of empty cardboard boxes beneath the lights.

PROVIDING AIR

 hen wind blows on plants and creates resistance, it makes them grow stronger. The air indoors, where you'll most likely be growing your microgreens, is relatively devoid of movement. To provide some semblance of resistance, consider thumbing gently through your microgreens, as you might the leaves of a book, once a day. In addition, electric fans can be used to help circulate the air and also guard against mold. This comes at a cost, of course: artificial wind saps electricity no less than does artificial light.

the inside scoop: germination and growth

- Rely on warmth for germination and light for growth.
- Use seedling heat mats or reptile heat mats to provide warmth during germination. Either type of mat can be affixed to the walls of a metal cabinet or glass aquarium to create an ideal germination space.
- Expect seeds to germinate much more quickly than predicted on seed packets.
- In cooler weather, expect members of the genus *Brassica* to thrive; others grow more slowly. Wait until spring to grow crops (such as basil) that don't do well in cool weather.
- Expose microgreens to at least ten hours of light and six hours of darkness each day.
- Use sufficient light to encourage growth of lush, sweet, green leaves and avoid development of long, bitter, and fibrous stems.
- For exposure to natural sunlight, grow microgreens either outdoors or indoors in front of a window; either way, take precautions to avoid heat damage.
- When growing microgreens indoors, augment with artificial light as necessary. Use either standard fluorescent or full-spectrum bulbs as electric grow lights.
- Create simple reflectors from cardboard or foam core board to enhance either natural or artificial light.

Sunflower: At right, four days darkness and two days continuous sunlight and artificial light. At left, two days darkness and four days only sunlight.

5

harvesting and storing

Whether you decide to grow microgreens in containers or trays (see chapters 6 and 7), the steps for harvesting and storing the greens are similar. The keys to success are knowing when to harvest the greens, what tools to use, where to snip the stems, and, as always, how to discourage bacteria or mold growth. And last but not least, knowing how to store the greens properly is another way of making all your efforts pay off.

SAY WHEN

The only way you'll know your greens are at their sweetest and most succulent point is to sample your crops every day. With each taste test, take notes about the plant's sweetness and also its texture. Is it still tender or is it becoming more fibrous? Keep track of the optimal harvest times for specific plants or batches of seeds during different seasons.

You'll likely find that microgreens reach optimal succulence during the seed leaf stage, before the second set of leaves (or true leaves) emerges. In general, most microgreens also taste sweeter when grown only to the seed leaf stage, when the leaves contain higher levels of phytonutrients. If you delay your harvest until after the true leaves have fully developed, your crop will be larger and taller, but it will also likely be slightly bitter and tough. (For more information about the seed leaf and true leaf stages, see chapter 1.)

Sampling the leaves before harvest is necessary because the above generalizations don't always apply. Some microgreens taste better when harvested at the true leaf stage. At this stage, for example, mustard greens are milder and most lettuces are less bitter. Some plants taste the same at both stages, but the texture may be less palatable at true leaf stage when plants become more fibrous.

Home growers can choose their harvest dates based on taste and succulence, whereas commercial growers must consider factors such as plant strength and volume. Most commercial microgreens are grown to true leaf stage because at seed leaf stage they look so similar to each other and are also too delicate for packing and shipping. Lettuce microgreens are especially fragile at both stages, which is why they're seldom grown or sold commercially. Plants at true leaf stage also pack more weight and fill more volume than those at seed leaf stage, which is a consideration for commercial growers.

REMOVING HULLS

You want to knock off as many of the hulls (or pods or shells) that cling to microgreen leaves before harvest as possible—and as gently as possible. It's much easier to spot and remove hulls while the microgreens are still firmly rooted in the soil, which provides leverage. If you delay this step until after harvest, the task will be more difficult.

Hulls are likely to stick on crops such as beet, chard, cilantro, fennel, fenugreek, radish, sunflower, and some varieties of lettuce. When it comes to hulls, other seedlings are in a class by themselves; in fact, hulls cling so tenaciously to spinach, this crop can't even be grown as a microgreen. (See sidebar, page 4.)

To get rid of hulls before harvest, hold the container or tray firmly above a trash can or sink, turn it until it's nearly vertical, and give the microgreens a "massage" by brushing the tops of the leaves gently with your fingers.

Some stubborn hulls will remain even after this procedure. Your options then are to either eat the hulls if they're soft or pick them off (one by one if necessary) if they're hard. Soft hulls, such as those on fennel, fenugreek, lettuce, and radish, can be eaten along with the leaves. These hulls are palatable and add a healthy dose of dietary fiber. Harder hulls, such as those on beet, chard, cilantro, and sunflower, are neither palatable nor safe to eat. They must be removed before the microgreens are consumed.

HARVESTING TOOLS

Compared to other types of gardening, microgreen gardening involves few tools. One essential piece of equipment, however, is a pair of sharp scissors. You should have one pair that you use solely for harvesting microgreens and for no other purpose.

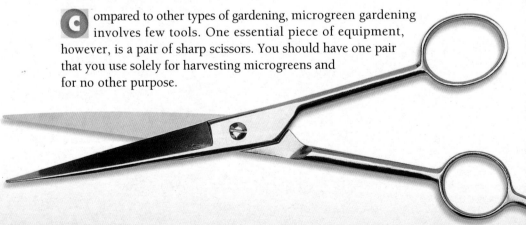

Using sharp scissors ensures a clean cut, and trimmed microgreens will keep for a longer period of time if the stems have been snipped cleanly. Jagged lacerations on the stems can lead to rot or bacterial growth, particularly on microgreens that are stored in the refrigerator and not eaten immediately.

Select scissors with long, sharp blades. A good place to find a wide selection of affordable scissors is an office supply store. Scissors constructed entirely of steel are easy to clean, whereas those with plastic-coated grips can be bothersome, especially if the plastic reaches to the joints. Some plastic grips feature an antimicrobial coating, which some gardeners may prefer.

You can also use gardening shears, which are sold in gardening stores, or herb snippers, which are sold in kitchen supply stores. However, neither is the ideal choice because these implements generally have long grips but short blades. On the plus side, some gardening shears (and some kitchen shears) have blades that disassemble for easy and effective cleaning.

wait for it: the welcome second wave

Delayed germination is nature's insurance policy against the eradication of a plant species due to poor growing conditions or crop failure. You'll experience some delayed germination when growing microgreens as well.

Many crops will have a second wave of late bloomers, when seeds that didn't yet germinate finally spring to life. For example, the second wave for arugula, basil, beet, marjoram, radish, and sunflower can be substantial and well worth the wait. Some seeds, such as sunflower, germinate for a third, fourth, and even fifth wave. For most species, though, the second crop will be meager.

In general, the larger the size of the seed, the greater the yield of its second wave. That explains why sunflower greens, which grow from large seeds, have many more waves than others. Radish, a *Brassica* that grows from comparatively large seeds, has a moderate second wave, while most other *Brassicas* (except for Asian mizuna) have next to none.

Most mucilaginous seeds (those that become sticky when wet), though tiny, produce respectable second waves, in part because the stiff film they form on the soil's surface delays the germination of seeds below the surface. Basil tops the list of mucilaginous seeds with worthy second waves, which is good to know in advance since basil seeds can be expensive. Understandably, gardeners may be more willing to pay for the seeds if they can expect a late wave with each crop.

Some seeds inevitably are late bloomers and take longer to germinate than others. Usually the delay is modest, perhaps only a week or slightly more, which explains the second wave in microgreen growth. In rare cases, however, seeds that are sown outdoors can germinate one full year later than those in the same batch.

You may also choose barber scissors, or shears, which are sold in pharmacies and salon supply stores. These shears have thin blades that work well for selective, piecemeal harvests. On the downside, they can be relatively expensive and you may only be able to find scissors with short blades.

Because scissors are an important tool in microgreen gardening, treat them with care and attention. After using the scissors to harvest microgreens, wipe the blades clean, then wash and dry the scissors.

HARVESTING TECHNIQUES

If you've grown microgreens in small containers, you're likely to harvest all the greens in one container at once. To do so, hold the container over a dish, tilt the container on its side, cut the stems with scissors (as close to the soil as possible), and the cuttings will fall into the dish.

If you're not ready to harvest all of the greens at once, use the same piecemeal technique you would use when harvesting microgreens in trays. (Chapters 6 and 7 provide more specific information about harvesting techniques used in container gardening or tray gardening.) Using scissors, trim the greens by patches or rows, leaving spaces into which the remaining greens can lean as they continue to grow.

For the first harvest, snip the stems *just above the soil*. If this is a partial harvest and you allow the remaining greens to grow for more than another week, mold might develop on the stubble in the harvested patches, and you want the mold to be as far from the unharvested greens as possible. To avoid mold, pull out the roots and any other remnants of the plants you've already harvested. Alternatively, interpret the first sign of mold as an indication that it's time to harvest the remaining crop.

When harvesting remaining greens, either from a partial harvest or a second wave, (see sidebar, page 31), you may want to snip the stems just below the leaves. This will help you avoid any mold that may have grown on the remnants of earlier harvests. Leaves taste better than stems in any case.

SKIP THE RINSE

If you've watered your microgreens (or more accurately, the soil) only from the bottom or the side, there shouldn't be any soil on the undersides of the stems or leaves. And if there's no soil, there should be no need to rinse your harvest.

You especially don't want to rinse microgreens if you plan to refrigerate them. Moisture increases the risk of rot, even for refrigerated greens. If you find that soil is clinging to the stems or leaves and want to rinse your microgreens, dry them thoroughly on a smooth towel or in a salad spinner before storing them in the refrigerator.

STORING YOUR MICROGREENS

One of the wonderful things about growing microgreens is that it's often possible to harvest the greens as you're ready to eat them. When this isn't the case, refrigerate whatever you don't plan to eat immediately.

The best way to store clipped greens is in a glass or food-safe plastic container with a lid. If necessary, it's okay to store microgreens in a bag if you handle the greens and bag gently. Set the refrigerator's thermostat close to the freezing point and you will keep your harvest fresh for two weeks or longer.

If you grow microgreens in repurposed containers (such as pints or half pints), you can refrigerate the greens, soil, container, and all if the greens are ready but you're not quite ready to eat them. After one week, the soil may need some soaking, after which the greens will remain fresh for yet another week. This is one of several conveniences that container gardening offers over tray gardening. For more tips about refrigerating greens in their containers, see the sidebar on page 43.

NOTE: There are two types of microgreens that should never be stored in the refrigerator. Avoid refrigerating amaranth and basil, both of which will turn to mush when exposed to cold.

save seeds and eat for free

It's easy to preserve your own seeds for growing microgreens. Transplant surplus seedlings outdoors during planting season, when conditions are optimal. When the plants grow to maturity, don't harvest them. Instead, let the plants go to seed and harvest the seeds. That way, you'll have the seeds you need to sow more microgreens, and you won't even have to glance at a seed catalog.

CLEANING UP—THE KEY TO CONTINUED SUCCESS

It's a good idea to develop a consistent cleanup routine after harvest. Even to the end, you must remain vigilant against the growth of bacteria or mold (one or the other may occur, but not both, since fungal growth suppresses bacterial growth). Here are some proven tips:

DISPOSE OF SOIL. After a full harvest, dispose of the root-entangled soil that remains in the containers or trays. If possible, dump the soil outdoors, where animal visitors will be happy to pick it clean for any remaining edibles.

CLEAN CONTAINERS AND TRAYS. Brush or shake off any soil deposits or root fragments, then allow the empty containers or trays to dry in the open air. If possible, put the containers or trays in direct sunlight in front of a sunny window; sunlight is an effective antiseptic. Give the containers or trays a rest, letting them remain empty and dry for several days between crops.

These steps should prevent bacteria or mold growth, but you may have reason to exercise greater caution, especially if you share your household with children, convalescents, or seniors, all of whom might be more vulnerable to illness. You can rinse your containers or trays with a dilute solution of white distilled vinegar (half water and half vinegar). If this doesn't prove effective, use an enzyme-based mold cleanser. If signs of mold persist, rinse the containers or trays with a dilute solution of hydrogen peroxide or—as a last resort—a dilute solution of bleach, which is what professional microgreen farmers use to rinse their seedling trays. Create a dilute bleach solution by combining at least nine parts water with one part bleach. The amount of dilution required for hydrogen peroxide depends on the concentration you're using. The common 3 percent solution is already mild, whereas a food-grade concentration of 35 percent requires significant dilution, similar to bleach.

SCRAPE AWAY THE STUBBORN BITS. No matter how carefully you harvest your microgreens, stems and leaves are likely to litter your kitchen counter or table and floor. This debris can be difficult to clean up, since it's moist and clings to dry surfaces. Try wiping with a cloth or sponge, wet or dry, and you may create more of a mess than before. Even worse, if you wait a while before cleaning up, the messy bits wither and dry out, which makes them stick even more.

One kitchen tool that's very useful at this stage is a food scraper, which is typically a sheet of stainless steel affixed to a plastic handle. The scraper's wide end is beveled like a knife, but only on one side, and the edge isn't as sharp as a knife's. Slide the scraper across the counter or table, and the scraps of microgreens will slide along with it and onto it, making it easy to dispose of them. Use a food scraper just once, and you're likely to consider it an indispensable indoor gardening tool forever.

the inside scoop: harvesting and storing

- Harvest microgreens when they're at their sweetest and most succulent. Taste the greens daily to know when they're at their peak.
- Just before harvesting, gently massage microgreens when they're still rooted in the soil to remove hulls, pods, or shells.
- Use sharp scissors with long blades to snip stems during harvest. Initially, trim the stems close to the soil. When completing partial harvests or harvesting second or subsequent waves, trim the stems close to the leaves.
- Avoid rinsing microgreens with water if they're not visibly soiled. If you must rinse, dry the microgreens completely before storing them in the refrigerator.
- Store clipped microgreens in a sealed container in the refrigerator.
- Clean and dry containers and trays between crops to discourage the growth of bacteria or mold. If necessary, use dilute solutions of vinegar, hydrogen peroxide, or bleach.
- For easy cleanup, use a food scraper to clear counters and tables of stems, leaves, and other debris.

planting in containers

Assembling the necessary equipment for container gardening can be simple and affordable if you repurpose certain types of food packaging. Clear plastic containers that hold berries, for example, work beautifully in microgreen gardening, but there are other options, including a few described in this chapter.

Repurposed containers are ideal for microgreen gardening because they're lightweight, versatile, and fit easily on most windowsills. The alternative to using repurposed food containers is to use trays (see chapter 7). The advantage of using trays is that you're able to grow more microgreens at once, but this efficiency comes with certain challenges. For one, trays can be cumbersome. It's easy to spill soil or drip water from a tray, for example. In addition, trays seldom fit on windowsills, which is a disadvantage if you don't have a large surface in front of a window.

As discussed in chapter 3, microgreens that are grown in containers are watered from the bottom. This involves putting containers that have holes in the bottom into shallow pools of water so that the water is absorbed directly into the soil from below. This watering method is the key to growing mold-free microgreens, and it's a topic that's explored further in this chapter. Microgreens that are grown in trays can't be watered from the bottom, although side watering is an option that can deter mold growth (see chapter 7).

One point worth noting here is that small containers have the advantage of providing somewhat more surface area because plants can lean outward and spread beyond the containers' perimeters, allowing you to fit in more seeds. In contrast, trays have tall lips and broad surface areas that don't allow expansion beyond their borders.

THE BEST CONTAINERS TO REPURPOSE

The containers that house fresh fruits are ideal for growing microgreens. Other common receptacles, such as those that are packed with hummus, tofu, or yogurt, are also good choices. As an alternative, you always have the option of purchasing plastic seedling pots from a garden supply store.

FRESH FRUIT CONTAINERS. Rather than immediately recycle the clear plastic containers in which you buy fresh fruits, wash and collect them. Stock up on empty pint (one-half kilo) and half-pint (one-quarter kilo) containers. Pint containers typically house blueberries, cherry tomatoes, and figs. Blackberries and raspberries come packaged in half-pint containers, which are half the depth but usually the same width and length as pints, making them particularly useful. Quart (one kilo) containers, such as those that hold strawberries, aren't a good choice for microgreen gardening, however, as they hold more soil than is necessary.

While either pint or half-pint containers will work no matter which seeds you plant, some seedlings do better in pint containers, which are twice as deep. In particular, pea and root crops, such as beet and radish, grow best in pint containers. For most other crops, and especially for shallow-rooted seedlings such as basil and lettuce, half-pint containers are preferred because they can be filled with half the amount of soil as pint containers. Keep in mind, though, that microgreens in half-pint containers must be watered more frequently. In comparison, microgreens in pint containers need to be watered less often because they're growing in twice the amount of soil.

Container depth matters because harvesting is easier when the container is filled with soil. When the soil line is even with the top of the container, you can efficiently snip the greens at the bottom of the stems, which would be hard to reach if the soil line were lower.

Plastic fruit containers have several features that make them ideal for container gardening. For one, they're rectangular, which makes it easy to line them up on a windowsill, shelf, or tray. For another, they're transparent, so they don't obstruct your view of the growing rootlets inside.

Finally, they already have vents cut into their bottoms, which means the holes that are needed for bottom watering are already there.

The vents, while convenient, present a slight drawback because the containers may splinter or crack along the vents after multiple uses. That's why it's a good idea to evaluate the condition of the containers after each harvest and recycle those that are worn out.

Pint and half-pint fruit containers are made of polyethylene terephthalate, the type of plastic (recycling number 1) that's also commonly used to make water and beverage bottles. When containers made of this material are exposed to heat or stored for prolonged periods, the phthalates can migrate into the containers' liquid contents. That's why you can detect the taste of plastic in bottled water, including bottled spring water, especially if it's transported from afar. At moderate room temperatures and for short durations, however, this type of plastic doesn't affect liquid or solid contents.

HUMMUS, TOFU, AND YOGURT CONTAINERS. These receptacles are especially suitable for repurposing. You can modify them for microgreen gardening by punching holes in their bottoms. One slight disadvantage of hummus or yogurt containers is their shape, which is usually round rather than square or rectangular, like tofu containers. Round containers have less surface area for growing than comparably sized square containers, and fewer round containers fit into the same space as square or rectangular containers.

Hummus, tofu, and yogurt are typically packaged in safer plastics (recycling numbers 2 and 5) that transmit no chemical residue to food contents. People who are particular about the plastic they use may prefer these containers to plastic fruit containers for this reason.

FLOWERPOTS AND SEEDLING POTS. Suitable nonfood containers include flowerpots and seedling pots. Plastic flowerpots work best, since terra-cotta pots are heavy, bulky, and fragile. Seedling pots are pint-sized plastic containers manufactured specifically for growing seedlings. Like plastic fruit containers, seedling pots are made of polyethylene (recycling number 1). They're inexpensive and can be purchased at well-stocked garden supply stores. Many commercial microgreen farmers use seedling pots.

PREPARING CONTAINERS

ou'll need to make a few easy alterations to your containers so they'll be suitable for microgreen gardening.

REMOVE LIDS. Since the lids of plastic fruit containers are joined to the bottoms on one side, you'll need to cut the lids off of these containers. Because plastic dulls blades, designate an old pair of scissors for this task; don't use the same pair you use to harvest microgreens. You may find it easier to trim off the lid if you turn the container upside down. After removing the lid, trim away any ragged edges. Set aside some of the lids for use during the early stage of germination of certain microgreens (see "Cover Up," page 41).

PUNCH HOLES. While plastic fruit containers are already vented and don't require this step, you'll need to punch holes in other food containers, such as those from hummus, tofu, and yogurt, and possibly even plastic flowerpots. To make the holes, turn the container upside down. Use a pointed knife or pick to create holes in the plastic. If the plastic is too dense, make the holes by tapping a sharp nail with a hammer to drive it through the plastic. To facilitate rapid watering and draining, punch numerous holes in every container.

NEST AND REINFORCE. Pair up identical containers and nest one inside the other. This is an important step. Doubling up the containers adds rigidity, strength, and stability so that fragile rootlets don't get jostled when you move the containers during watering or another step. Plus, by nesting one container inside of another, you create a buffer zone that protects the rootlets in the inner container from being crushed, prevents water from pooling in the soil, and provides ventilation (which prevents mold).

LINE WITH PAPER. Line the bottom of the inside container with a piece of thin white paper, such as printer paper, before adding soil. To cut the paper to the correct size, place the container top-side down on a sheet of paper (or on a piece of cardboard if you want to make a reusable template), trace around the container with a pen or pencil to mark its outline on the paper, and cut a bit outside the outline with scissors. Then, starting from each of the four corners, snip a short incision diagonally toward the center. Firmly insert the paper into the bottom of the container, allowing the paper to come slightly up the sides; make sure the insert fits snugly.

Lining the top container with paper has a twofold purpose. While the primary goal is to prevent soil from draining into the water during bottom watering, the paper also prevents rootlets from entangling themselves in container

Basil, from day 1 to day 6.

vents and holes. This will make it easier to clean and reuse your containers.

GROW YOUR GARDEN

Now that the containers are lid-free, have adequate holes in the bottom, and are nested together for stability, it's time to make a garden out of them by adding soil and seeds. For most crops, the simple sowing directions that follow will cover all you need to know. However, if you're growing sunflower, pea, or wheatgrass, refer to chapter 8, which provides more specific instructions for successfully growing those microgreens.

FILL THE CONTAINER WITH SOIL. Scoop moistened soil (see chapter 3, page 17) into the container. Don't pack down the soil, but do fill it right up to the rim. Filling the container to the top is important because it's much easier to harvest the microgreens when the soil line is even with the container's rim.

MEASURE THE SEEDS. Here is a cheat sheet that can help you determine the amount of seeds to sow in a pint or half-pint container. This step is optional if you're using seeds that don't require soaking, but it's helpful to keep a record of how many seeds to use per container. The lengths and widths of pint and half-pint containers vary only slightly among manufacturers, so their total surface areas average about eighteen square inches (116 square centimeters). Here are the *maximum* amounts of seeds you'll need per pint or half-pint container:

- tiny seeds (such as basil)   = maximum ½ teaspoon (2.5 milliliters)
- medium seeds (such as broccoli) = maximum 1 teaspoon (5 milliliters)
- large seeds (such as radish)   = maximum 1½ teaspoons (7.5 milliliters)
- extra-large seeds (such as beet) = maximum 2 teaspoons (10 milliliters)

Broccoli, from day 1 to day 6.

SOW THE SEEDS. Lay the seeds evenly and thinly upon the soil. Deep-bowled measuring spoons are excellent tools not just for measuring seeds, but also for sowing them: hold the spoon with your thumb and middle finger and gently tap the handle with your forefinger to sow the seed.

Only seeds that have been soaked should be covered with soil (see sidebar, "To Soak or Not to Soak," page 10, for a list of seeds that require soaking). For all *except* soaked seeds, use your fingers to gently press the seeds into the soil, ensuring contact but not covering the seeds with soil. This will prevent succulent leaves from being encrusted with soil as the seedlings emerge and grow.

LABEL THE CONTAINER. Write the seed's name on a label and affix it to the container (small labels the size of address labels work perfectly). Also inscribe the date that the seeds were sown; this notation will help you track the number of days you prefer to grow each variety of microgreen.

COVER UP. Until the seeds germinate, cover the soil and seeds with cloth (see chapter 3, pages 19 to 20) or even a bit of wet paper towel. If you're growing one of the few seeds that require light to fully germinate, don't use cloth or paper; instead, use the lid from the food container. Fruit container tops are already vented, but if you're using other kinds of food containers, punch some holes in them. It's not necessary to snap on the lid; simply place it atop the container. You might prefer to dispense with cloth covers altogether and instead cover only with lids. If you would rather not cover the containers even with lids, the seeds can be left uncovered as long as you mist or spray them three times daily.

WATER FROM THE BOTTOM

T he technique of watering plants from below is adapted from a method used by large-scale microgreen farmers, who deliver their uncut crops to restaurants and markets still in their seedling containers. The microgreens continue to grow in the restaurant and the marketplace—and they do so without becoming moldy. Avoiding mold is the main goal of bottom watering. Water your microgreens whenever the top of the soil feels dry, usually once daily for half-pint containers and every other day for pint containers, which are deeper.

PREPARE A SHALLOW POOL OF WATER. Pour room-temperature water into a bowl, basin, or small tub until the water is about half as deep as the container of microgreens you'll be watering. Don't use cold water because it will chill the roots and delay their growth.

PLACE THE CONTAINER INTO THE WATER. The numerous vent holes in the bottom of the container allow for soaking now and for draining later. Let the soil soak up water for one minute or less, until the surface of the soil feels thoroughly moistened. Then remove the container from the water.

DRAIN THE EXCESS WATER. Allow the container to drain for one minute or more by setting it at a slight angle inside the sink or dish rack.

REPLENISH THE WATER AS NEEDED. If you're watering more than four containers of microgreens, you'll need to add water to the pool as it's soaked up. Watering containers one at a time takes longer than watering four simultaneously in a large basin, which is a practical approach if you grow a lot of microgreens. A clean dishpan works well for most people, but enthusiastic growers who like to reuse all kinds of containers might be interested to learn that a repurposed drawer from an old refrigerator can hold six containers at a time.

DISCARD LEFTOVER WATER. If you didn't line the container with paper as directed earlier in this chapter (see page 39), some soil may remain behind in the watering basin when you're finished. This is especially likely to occur early in the growing cycle, before rootlets emerge. If you pour heavily soiled water down the sink, over time, the soil might clog the drain. One solution is to pour the water into the sink through a sprout-jar lid with a fine mesh screen, which will catch the soil. Alternatively, the soil and water can be discarded outdoors.

HARVESTING FROM CONTAINERS

C hapter 5 includes general information about harvesting microgreens. Here are some additional details that pertain to harvesting greens grown in containers.

HARVEST BUT DON'T WASH. Small containers allow for an easy and efficient harvest. Since the harvest per container is likely to be small, you'll probably want to trim away all of the greens at once. To do so, hold the container over a

refrigerate the whole operation

If you grow microgreens in repurposed containers, you have the unique option of refrigerating the micro-greens *before* harvest. If your greens are at their sweet peak but you're not yet ready to eat them, simply put the container—soil and all—in the refrigerator. Because the cold air will dry out the plants, first put the container in a plastic bag, which you can leave open or tie loosely closed. For good measure, give the plants a little extra carbon dioxide by exhaling into the bag before tying it closed. The carbon dioxide will help to preserve the greens. If stored for one week with the bag open, the soil will dry out, so replenish moisture by bottom watering. You then can store it in the fridge for one more week. When you're nearly ready to eat the greens, remove the container from the refrigerator and put it on the windowsill. Let the container sit for twelve hours before trimming so the microgreens reach room temperature.

dish, tilt the container on its side, snip the stems with scissors, and the cuttings will fall into the dish. You need not even touch the microgreens, so they should be quite clean. In addition, because they've been watered from the bottom, the microgreens should be devoid of soil, and they shouldn't need to be washed.

HARVEST IN PATCHES. If you prefer to harvest only some of the greens growing in the container, trim them by patches or rows, leaving spaces into which the remaining greens can lean as they continue to grow. This harvesting technique is commonly used in tray gardening.

CUT LOW DOWN THE STEMS. What if you didn't follow the earlier advice to fill the soil to the top of the container? This may or may not be a problem, depending on how far down the stem you prefer to cut. If you want to harvest as much stem as possible, but you didn't fill the container to the rim, the stems are now deep inside the container and difficult to reach with scissors. But there's a simple solution, especially if you've used softer, more flexible containers, such as fruit or tofu containers. Simply remove the inner container from the outer protective container. With one hand, loosely hold the microgreen container by its sides, and with your other hand, push up the bottom of the container. The matted clump of soil will slide up. When the surface of the soil is even with the edge of the container, snip the stems close to the soil line.

DISCARD THE SOIL. After a full harvest, hold the container upside down. Give the bottom a slight nudge, and the cluster of root-entangled soil will slide out as a single mass. If loose soil remains in the container, that's a sign that you may have used more soil than necessary. For example, if you used a pint container, the next time you grow the same variety of microgreen, use a half-pint container instead.

Some rootlets may cling to the bottom of the container, especially if they're tangled in the vents. To dislodge these, scrub and wash the container. If absolutely necessary, immerse the container in a sink filled with water to soak and loosen the roots.

the inside scoop: container gardening

- Repurpose food containers such as pint or half-pint containers that hold fruit or other containers that hold hummus, tofu, or yogurt.
- Use flowerpots or seedling pots for container gardening if you prefer or if you don't have enough empty food containers to reuse.
- Prepare containers by removing lids, punching holes in the bottoms, nesting one container inside another, and lining the bottom of the inside container with paper.
- When it's time to plant, fill the container to the rim with moist soil, sow the appropriate amount of seeds for the size of the container, and lay the seeds evenly and thinly upon the soil. (Don't cover the seeds with soil unless they have been soaked.)
- Label each container with the name of the seed and the planting date.
- After germination, water the microgreens only from the bottom.
- Harvest the microgreens by clipping the stems close to the soil. Don't wash the clippings.
- Put unharvested microgreens in a bag, container and all, and store in the refrigerator until you're ready to eat them. (Allow them to come to room temperature for twelve hours before harvesting.)

Green Cabbage and Chinese Cabbage

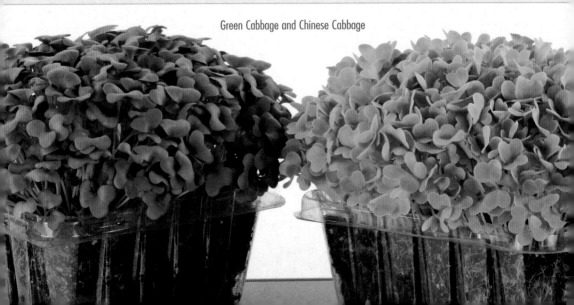

planting in trays

With tray gardening you'll use either shallow cafeteria trays (also called fast-food trays) or deeper seedling trays (also called nursery flats). In the early days of homegrown microgreens, growers often used commercially manufactured seedling trays and watered their crops from above. Today, the better option is to use cafeteria trays, which are much easier to manage and can be watered from the side to avoid mold growth.

Any microgreen that can be grown in small, repurposed food containers can also be grown in trays. The advantage of tray gardening, of course, is greater yields. This chapter contains information about using either cafeteria trays or seedling trays to grow microgreens.

CAFETERIA TRAYS

Y ou might be able to find a cafeteria manager (or the director of dining services) at a school or college who is willing to give away old trays. If you decide to purchase new cafeteria trays, you can buy them from a restaurant supply store or online source. In addition, some sprouting supply companies stock cafeteria trays, so you can order both trays and microgreen seeds from the same source. Consider buying a multipack when you shop. Even if you find you prefer to plant in containers, the trays can be used to support and transport repurposed food containers.

When buying trays from restaurant supply vendors, you can choose from an array of sizes, colors, and materials. If you have the option, select several small, white (white reflects the most light) polypropylene cafeteria trays. Ideally, you want trays that you can lay flat inside your kitchen sinks.

Cafeteria trays are fabricated from many synthetic materials, including acrylic, fiberglass, polycarbonate,

instead of plastic

If you shun synthetics, you can grow microgreens in rimmed stainless steel baking sheets or serving platters instead of plastic trays. However, when it's in constant contact with moist soil, stainless steel does stain and will rust, so your equipment eventually will need to be replaced: Plastic trays, on the other hand, will last a lifetime.

polypropylene, and polystyrene, and all of these may display the seal of approval from NSF International, a certifier of food service equipment. But not all are equally safe for microgreen gardening. Polycarbonate contains bisphenol A (BPA), which is known to migrate into food contents, so avoid trays made of this material. The most stable and therefore safest choice is polypropylene, and the strongest is fiberglass.

Whichever type of cafeteria tray you choose, you need at least two trays to make a set: a bottom tray to fill with soil and a top one to serve as its cover. You may even need a third tray if the trays aren't thick and sturdy, because some low-priced trays are almost half as thick as others and too flimsy to use alone. The danger of using wobbly trays is that fragile rootlets could be jostled. If necessary, double up two thin trays to use in place of one bottom tray, in which case you'll need three trays per set.

Grow Your Garden

It's time to create your tray garden by adding soil and seeds. This section includes general instructions that pertain to most microgreens. However, if you're growing sunflower, pea, or wheatgrass, refer to chapter 8, which provides more specific instructions for growing these microgreens.

MEASURE THE SEEDS. It's only necessary to measure seeds if you're going to soak them, but it's also helpful to do it just because you want to establish a specific seed count per tray. Here's a very simple method for determining the amount of seeds to sow per cafeteria tray. Spread a single layer of seeds in a cafeteria tray when it's empty, before you fill it with soil. Allow enough room between seeds so that none touch each other. Next, gather the seeds off the tray, measure them, and record the amount. Refer to this amount not only for this crop but also for all future crops grown from the same seeds in the same size cafeteria trays.

FILL THE CAFETERIA TRAY WITH SOIL. Scoop moistened soil (see chapter 3, page 17) into the tray and spread the soil evenly. Cafeteria trays are shallow, never taller than one inch (2.5 centimeters) and rarely even that high. So, fill the tray with soil all the way to the rim. Flatten the soil, but you need not be obsessive about it. If you like, sculpt a slight central mound that gently slopes toward the edges and dig an irrigation ditch around the tray's edges. This will facilitate drainage during side watering.

SOW THE SEEDS. Lay the seeds evenly and thinly upon the soil. Deep-bowled measuring spoons are excellent tools not just for measuring seeds, but also for sowing them: hold the spoon with your thumb and middle finger and gently tap the handle with your forefinger to sow the seed.

Only seeds that have been soaked should be covered with soil (see sidebar, "To Soak or Not to Soak," page 10, for a list of seeds that require soaking). For all *except* soaked seeds, use your fingers to gently press the seeds into the soil, ensuring contact but not covering the seeds with soil. This will prevent succulent leaves from being encrusted with soil as the seedlings emerge and grow.

LABEL THE CAFETERIA TRAY. Write the seed's name on a label and affix it to the tray (small labels the size of address labels work perfectly). Also inscribe the date that the seeds were sown; this notation will help you track the number of days you prefer to grow each variety of microgreen.

COVER UP. Until the seeds germinate, cover the cafeteria tray that contains the soil and seeds with an inverted tray. If you lack an extra tray, a wet hand towel or even wet newspaper can serve as a cover. If you're growing one of the few seeds that require light to fully germinate, don't use a cover unless it's transparent. One option is to use the see-through plastic dome covers that are sold with seedling trays. If you prefer not to cover the seeds, they can be left uncovered as long as you mist or spray them three times daily.

Water from the Side

Microgreens that are grown in cafeteria trays can't be watered from the bottom, and they certainly shouldn't be watered from above. Instead, an alternative method of hydration, namely side watering, is required. Watering from the side discourages the growth of mold as effectively as bottom watering. One daily watering usually is sufficient.

WATER INSIDE THE SINK. Tilt the cafeteria tray and put it inside the sink, short-side down, and position it so that one end of the tray is resting inside the sink and the other against the edge of the sink. Using the sink's pull-out sprayer hose (adjust the nozzle to create a narrow stream) or a watering can (choose one with a narrow spout), pour only a trickle of water directly into the soil, not onto the greens, at the top of the tray. Continue to water until the soil in the middle of the tray is moistened, then rotate the tray until the dry end is at the top. Repeat the process. If the tray is small enough to fit inside the sink, you can prop it up on its long sides and adapt this method to water from all four sides rather than only two.

DRAIN THE EXCESS WATER. When the soil is fully moistened across its entire surface, let the cafeteria tray remain tilted inside the sink for at least five minutes to allow the excess water to drain.

TRY A VARIATION ON BOTTOM WATERING. Once microgreens have grown in a cafeteria tray for several days, their roots form a mat with the soil. When this happens, you can lift the edge of the mat slightly off the tray and pour water directly into the tray. In this way, you can simulate the bottom-watering method used for containers, in which the soil absorbs water from below.

Reap What You Sow

Chapter 5 included general information about harvesting microgreens. Here are some additional details that relate to harvesting greens grown in cafeteria trays.

HARVEST BATCHES IN PATCHES. When you grow microgreens in cafeteria trays, you can harvest the entire crop in one swoop, but you aren't likely to eat all the greens in a single meal. Instead of storing leftovers in the refrigerator, the better idea is to harvest patches or rows of microgreens rather than the whole tray.

Using scissors, cut central paths along the length and along the width of the tray to create a cross-like pattern. This thinning out technique is a standard gardening practice that provides unharvested plants more room to grow. (Within a few days, the microgreens in the remaining quadrants will lean into the open pathways and nearly cover them.) The next day or for your next meal, cut one or two new paths through each quadrant. Allow your checkerboard another day or two of growth. Harvest that and you'll be done with the entire tray.

DON'T WASH. Like microgreens that have been watered from the bottom, those that have been watered from the side should be devoid of soil, and they shouldn't need to be washed. Microgreens are only likely to be soiled if they're watered from above or if they're exposed to rainfall. To remove soil, home gardeners must rinse the greens after harvest, and it's very difficult to completely dry microgreens after they've been rinsed. The extra handling and remaining dampness severely shorten their shelf life, even when microgreens are refrigerated.

SEEDLING TRAYS

Many professional microgreen farmers grow their crops in seedling trays, the long, deep trays that are also known as nursery flats. These large trays provide an advantage in that they allow a lot of growing space; however, because they're unwieldy, they're an impractical choice for home growers. Also, bottom watering and side watering aren't feasible options, so the trays have to be watered from above. This promotes mold and rot and leads to crop loss.

Unless you're willing to install a hothouse and construct an elaborate watering, drainage, and air circulation setup just to grow microgreens, you'll likely decide against using large, cumbersome seedling trays. For the ambitious home grower, however, information about growing microgreens in seedling trays follows. In comparison to using cafeteria trays, preparation and watering are quite different, although sowing and harvesting are similar. (See the previous section for sowing and harvesting tips.)

Prepare a Set

Assembling a set of seedling trays requires a bit more effort than using cafeteria trays. It also can cost more, since you're unlikely to obtain donated or free seedling trays.

BUY THE SEEDLING TRAYS (NURSERY FLATS). From a gardening store, buy three plastic seedling trays and one matching transparent plastic dome cover. If the cover is not available, purchase a fourth seedling tray instead.

PUNCH HOLES. The seedling trays that you buy may already have drainage holes in them. If not, you're likely to get trays that are manufactured with indentations that you can puncture to make drainage holes. Don't be timid— go ahead and punch holes throughout the length of two (but not all three) trays. On one short side only, make many extra holes in both trays. Water needs to flow, not just drip, through this end of the trays, as it will sit in your sink when you elevate the other end.

ASSEMBLE A SET. Nest the two seedling trays (both should have holes) together, one inside the other. Make sure that the short sides with the extra holes are at the same end. Put the two nested trays into a third tray that has no holes. This bottom tray should be removed during watering. After watering, it should be placed back under the two nested trays to collect any water that might continue to drain.

CREATE A SUPPORT. When filled with soil, especially moistened soil, seedling trays become very heavy and unstable. Seedling trays typically are two inches (five centimeters) high and will hold more soil than is needed for most microgreens, especially those grown only to seed leaf stage. You have little choice but to fill the trays almost to the rim with soil; otherwise, cutting the microgreens low on the stem during harvest can be very awkward.

You must create a support for the heavy trays to ensure that the roots won't be jostled as you transport the trays from the sunny window to the kitchen sink. To make a support, cut a 10 x 20-inch (25 x 50-centimeter) piece of cardboard or foam core, or even better, saw a piece of plywood that size. (This will fit the most common-size tray.) Place the support under the set of trays whenever you transport it.

RETAIN MOISTURE. Finally, place the transparent plastic dome cover (or fourth tray) on top of the three nested seedling trays. The cover will help to retain moisture during the germination stage. For the few seeds that require darkness to more fully germinate, a fourth seedling tray, when inverted, can provide darkness.

Water from the Top

You can't water microgreens that are grown in seedling trays from the side because the lips of the trays are too tall. And because the trays are too large, you can't water seedling trays from the bottom by putting them inside

the kitchen sink. You can try bottom watering elsewhere, such as in the bathtub, but that's impractical on a daily basis; water is likely to drip throughout the house as you transfer the trays from the tub to their growing location. That leaves one option when growing microgreens in seedling trays: top watering.

WATER THE TRAYS IN THE SINK. Remove the bottom tray (the tray with no holes in it). Tilt the nested trays and put them into the sink, positioning the trays so that the short side with the many holes is inside the sink; the opposite end will extend outside of the sink. Water the microgreens from above using the sink's pull-out sprayer hose if the stream is gentle enough or with a watering can equipped with a sprinkler head. Continue until the soil is moistened.

DRAIN THE EXCESS WATER. After watering, leave the trays in the sink for at least five minutes; because the trays will only fit in the sink at an angle, the resulting incline will ensure drainage. Get out some towels and clear the kitchen counter of the misdirected water, as there's likely to be some (or perhaps quite a bit). Then transfer the trays onto a cloth towel to absorb any moisture that may remain. Next, place the two nested trays back into the dry third tray (the tray with no holes) and return the entire setup to its place in front of a sunny window or beneath a grow light.

the inside scoop: tray gardening

- Obtain used cafeteria trays by requesting them from a school or college cafeteria. Alternatively, buy a new multipack of trays from a restaurant supply vendor. Opt for small, white, polypropylene trays if you have the option.
- Use stainless steel trays (such as rimmed baking sheets) if you prefer not to use plastic trays. Eventually, the stainless steel will rust and need to be replaced.
- Determine the amount of seeds to plant per cafeteria tray by spreading a single layer of seeds in an empty tray. The seeds shouldn't touch each other.
- When it's time to plant, fill the cafeteria tray to the rim with moist soil, sow the appropriate amount of seeds for the size of the tray, and lay the seeds evenly and thinly upon the soil. (Don't cover the seeds with soil unless they have been soaked.)
- Label each tray with the name of the seed and the planting date.
- During the germination stage, cover the cafeteria tray full of seeds with an inverted tray unless the seeds require light for germination (few do).
- Water microgreens grown in cafeteria trays from the side.
- Harvest microgreens in batches since you won't be likely to eat an entire tray of microgreens at one meal. Don't wash the microgreens.
- As an alternative to growing in cafeteria trays, grow microgreens in seedling trays, which are larger and deeper. The downside is that the full trays are heavy and unwieldy, and the microgreens must be watered from above, which promotes mold growth.

8

growing sunflower and pea microgreens

In part because they're resistant to mold, sunflower and pea microgreens have been popular choices for decades. These crops discourage mold growth because their stems are thick but their canopies aren't, which means the leaves don't trap and hold water even when they're watered from above. Sunflower seeds are large, which makes it harder to sow them too closely together, thereby preventing a thick canopy of leaves. Peas grow sparsely distributed leaves that amount to hardly any canopy.

Sunflower and pea microgreens all flourish when grown in either cafeteria trays or seedling trays. Because of the popularity of these microgreens, this chapter features specific details for how to grow them effectively.

SUNFLOWER GREENS

The very idea of growing and eating sunflower greens began with one person, Viktoras Kulvinskas, cofounder of the Hippocrates Health Institute. A treat among microgreens, sunflower demands and deserves special attention.

Successfully growing sunflower greens means employing several techniques that aren't recommended for most other microgreen crops. For example, the seeds are germinated inside a sprouting jar after soaking, the soaked seeds are *not* covered with soil, the emerging rootlets are covered with a weighted tray to encourage them to head down into the soil, and the greens are watered from above, which softens the shells and makes it easier for the leaves to shuck them off. In fact, the downside to growing sunflower greens is that some gardeners may tire of plucking the inedible shells off the leaves. However, if you follow the steps outlined in this chapter, you'll be ensured a harvest in which no (or at least very few) annoying shells cling to the tender sunflower leaves.

This chapter features specific details for how to grow sunflower greens effectively. The following instructions will tell you how to proceed by the hour and the day.

Choosing Your Seeds

The best seeds to use to grow sunflower greens are black oil sunflower seeds in their shells, the same seeds that are used to make sunflower oil. Sprouting and garden seed suppliers sell black oil seeds exclusively for growing sunflower greens. These retailers often stock seeds that have been bred for the specific trait of shedding shells. Generally, such seeds are very small and their shells are dark black and shiny.

If you find a source of high-quality seeds, consider reordering a large supply immediately and store the seeds in the refrigerator. In their shells, black oil sunflower seeds retain their viability for a long time.

When it comes to growing greens, black oil sunflower seeds offer a distinct advantage over the striped variety, which are mostly grayish black with thin white stripes. The sunflower kernels that we eat as snacks come from striped seeds, which are far larger than black oil seeds and also produce larger greens. But bigger isn't always better: the striped shells are dense and thick and cling to leaves more tenaciously than the black shells. If you grow sunflower greens from striped seeds, you're sure to lose patience since you'll have to pluck off nearly all of the striped shells by hand.

You might wager that you can win this "shell game" by starting with sunflower seeds that have already been removed from their shells, but hulled seeds aren't recommended for growing sunflower greens. Hulled, the seeds quickly lose viability unless they're refrigerated, yet neither distributors nor sellers refrigerate them. If you were to try growing seeds from six or seven local or mail-order sources, you would be fortunate if just one batch of hulled seeds germinated at a rate greater than 90 percent. Many batches don't germinate at all.

Birds especially like black oil sunflower seeds because they have a high oil content and are easy to shell. Unhulled sunflower seeds intended for wild bird feed can be used for growing sunflower greens because they sprout well, and this option may be of interest to people who are particularly frugal or live on a limited income. The downside is that the seeds come with all sorts of debris, which may include insect eggs that "sprout" into larvae. Seeds intended for human consumption are more carefully sifted and culled.

Grow Your Greens

Sunflower thrives in summer heat or in warmly heated homes, but germination and growth slacken in cool temperatures. Depending on the season, your results when growing sunflower greens at home may vary. The timeline below is based on growth patterns in early summer, when noontime temperatures average 80 degrees F (27 degrees C). **Note:** Be sure to label the tray with the sowing date and keep notes throughout the process to document your own timeline.

HOUR ZERO: Measure the seeds. There's no one-size-fits-all recommendation for the amount of black oil sunflower seeds to sow per cafeteria tray because the seeds vary in size and so do the trays. But here's a potential starting point: use ½ cup (118 milliliters) of seeds, which is a suitable amount of average-sized seeds to fill an average-sized tray.

Another option is to measure the surface area of the soil in the cafeteria tray. For every 100 square inches (645 square centimeters), use no more than 4½ tablespoons (66 milliliters) of seeds. If you prefer to avoid calculations, follow the instructions for measuring on page 40.

As described in the next step, sunflower seeds must be soaked before sowing. Therefore, they must be measured before they're soaked. But what if you sow the seeds and find you have measured and soaked too few? You can fill the remaining bare soil with a different variety of microgreen seed that doesn't need soaking but germinates and grows at the same rate as sunflower. Napa cabbage is a good choice. Or, if you have soaked too many sunflower seeds, you can sow the excess in a pint (one-half kilo) container or two. Or just feed the soaked seeds to the birds. They'll appreciate the free lunch and especially the softened shells.

HOURS ZERO TO 8: Soak the seeds. Put the measured seeds into a one-quart (about one-liter) widemouthed jar. A glass canning jar is a good choice, but any jar will do. Fill the jar with water and let the seeds soak for eight hours at room temperature. If you soak the seeds for eight hours, you can accelerate microgreen growth by twenty-four hours. The timing need not be exact: soaking the seeds between four hours and twelve hours is okay too. If you're pressed for time, soaking the seeds for only one or two hours is better than not soaking them at all.

As the black shells soak and their natural colors are released, the soak water will rapidly become cloudy. Your goal is to keep the water clear, which means changing the water. To facilitate draining, screw a sprouting jar strainer lid on to the jar and pour out the water. If you don't have such a lid, an alternative is to use pliable nylon screen or cheesecloth, either of which can be affixed to the jar with a rubber band. Another option is to pour the water through a fine-mesh strainer or colander. Once the cloudy water has been drained, refill the jar with fresh water, stir or swish the seeds around in the jar, then let it stand. If the shells continue to stain the water, repeat this procedure as often as is convenient. However, if you're able to freshen the water only once midway through the soak cycle, that's sufficient.

OPTIONAL: Make a plunger. Unhulled sunflower seeds float, so some of the seeds that you're soaking are likely to rise slightly above the waterline, like the tip of an iceberg. These seeds won't be properly soaked and won't germinate uniformly with the others. To avoid this problem, create a plunger that will keep all the seeds under water. Simply trim a piece of stiff nylon screen or a lid from a plastic container to fit snugly against the inside walls of the jar. Put the plunger inside the jar on top of the seeds and push it down. If the plunger is sized correctly, it will keep all the seeds fully and uniformly submerged. But if the plunger is slightly loose, seeds can escape and float to the top of the water. To prevent this, weigh down the plunger with a spoon or another utensil.

HOUR 8: Drain the water. To give the seeds a final rinse, refill the jar with fresh water and drain that water too.

HOURS 8 TO 32: Germinate the seeds. You have the option of germinating the seeds (allowing them to sprout) for twenty-four hours before sowing. If you prefer not to sprout the seeds, however, you can simply sow the soaked seeds.

Germinating the seeds offers four advantages. First, the shells will soften as the seeds are rinsed, which will make it easier for the greens to shuck off the shells as they grow. Second, it's easier to keep the seeds warm in a jar than in the soil. Third, the warmth and rinsing will accelerate growth. And fourth, sprouting a batch of seeds in advance, particularly if you're using a new variety of seed, allows you to verify a promising germination rate before sowing. If the germination rate is low, you can discard the seeds before sowing them and avoid wasting any soil.

To germinate the seeds, put them into a jar or any sprouting container of your choice. Cover the jar with a sprouting jar strainer lid or a piece of screen or cheesecloth, as described in the soaking step (page 54). Keep the seeds warm, at least at room temperature. (Sunflowers are summer crops, so the warmer the better.) If temperatures are cool, you may need to allow the seeds to germinate for twice as long.

Rinse the seeds at least twice during the germination period, and more frequently if convenient. After each rinsing, ensure that air can flow into the jar by tapping the screen in the lid to dislodge any droplets of water. Set the jar on its side and angle it slightly downward so that any remaining water drains. Leaning the jar inside a bowl often provides the desired angle, plus the bowl catches the drainage.

HOUR 32: Give the seeds one final rinse. At about this time, a white rootlet, called the radicle, should begin to poke through the tip of the shell. This miracle of birth is particularly stunning when it involves sunflower seeds; the seeds' large size and the high contrast between the white rootlets and black shells make the spectacle quite dramatic.

Now that the rootlets have emerged, rinse the sprouted seeds one last time before sowing. If necessary, you can postpone sowing the seeds for one more day, but no longer. If you wait too long, the rootlets will begin to bend, and after tumbling about with each rinsing, they'll point in many different directions, preventing them from properly taking root in the soil.

DAY 1 PLUS 8 HOURS: Sow and mist the seeds. Spread the seeds evenly upon the tray of moistened soil. Don't allow the seeds to rest on top of each other, or they'll rot instead of taking root. Press the seeds deeply into the soil, but don't cover them with soil. This is the exception to the rule, because soaked seeds are usually covered with soil, which makes it easier for the emerging plants to lose their shells. Inexplicably, covering sunflower seeds with soil only makes the shells cling to emerging leaves more tenaciously, maybe because dried soil acts like mortar and cements the hulls to the leaves.

After sowing the seeds, spray them with water. Use a spray bottle or mister for this task, not the sink's pull-out spray hose, because the stream is likely to be too forceful and might disturb or move the seeds. Use enough water to thoroughly moisten the soil, but don't use so much that puddles form.

DAY 1 PLUS 8 HOURS: Cover the tray. Put an empty cafeteria tray on top of the seeds so that the tray's bottom rests directly on the seeds. If you can provide a top tray that's larger than the one on the bottom, all the better, but the same size tray will suffice. Now press down on the top tray. As long as the soil isn't oversaturated, enough air will reach the seeds to promote growth.

This step is necessary because sunflower seeds quickly lose their vigor. They send forth their rootlets, but the rootlets may lack the energy to take root. If they fail to burrow into the soil, the rootlets will wander aimlessly on top of it. The top tray nudges them in the right direction.

DAYS 2 TO 3: Keep the seeds covered, check daily, and spray if needed. Once a day, gently remove the top tray to take a peek. If the seeds and soil appear parched, spray away, although the seeds won't likely need to be sprayed until day 3.

On day 3, the rootlets will begin to anchor themselves into the soil. Soon after, the seedlings will begin to lift the top tray. Though only slight, the gap that's widening between the two trays will provide a clear sign that your plans for a bountiful harvest have taken root.

DAYS 3 TO 4: Spray as needed and add weight. Once a day, remove the top tray and spray with water as needed. After you return the top tray, put some weight on it to encourage vigorous growth. The specific amount of weight isn't important. For example, put the spray bottle, the empty sprout jar, several more empty trays, or another tray filled with soil and sunflower seeds on top of the first tray. This added resistance straightens and strengthens both the stems and the roots. If the sunflower seeds have strong vigor, the added weight isn't needed. But such resistance can neither hurt nor hinder the seeds, so you might as well add some weight.

DAY 4 OR 5: Remove the weight and redirect misguided seedlings. Take off the top tray and any added weight before the gap between the two trays widens to one inch (2.5 centimeters). While the tray is off, pluck away any misguided seedlings using fine tweezers (not your fingers). Misguided seedlings include those that are blocked by other seedlings from making contact with the soil, have failed to anchor their roots, or have grown in a direction other than down into the soil. If you don't remove the wayward seedlings, they'll die, rot, and contaminate the healthy seedlings. This step can be a little tricky; avoid uprooting anchored seedlings whose roots have become entangled with unanchored seedlings.

DAY 4 OR 5: Expose the seedlings to light. Expose the sunflower greens to light if possible on day 4, otherwise surely by day 5. To grow lush leaves rather than long stems, provide the greens with as much direct sunlight as the season allows. Consider moving the tray outdoors so the greens are exposed to sunlight that isn't filtered by glass or even a window screen. Direct sunlight broadens, thickens, and energizes the leaves so significantly that they pop off nearly all the shells after merely one day in the sun. Just beware of roving squirrels and skydiving blue jays who are attracted to the shells and seek a tasty treat.

It's worth mentioning here that many large-scale microgreen farmers don't expose sunflower greens to light at this stage; rather, they continue to keep their seedlings in the dark, which yields long stems and paltry leaves. Some farmers expose the greens to light only on the final day, which explains why their pale sunflower greens taste like iceberg lettuce.

DAYS 5 TO 7: Top water daily. It's time to give your trigger finger a rest. The roots that previously might have been dislodged by more than a gentle misting are now securely anchored, so you can shower the sunflower greens from above with a watering can or a pull-out sprayer hose at the sink.

Put the tray of sunflower greens flat on the bottom of the sink if it fits; if not, tilt the tray so that one end rises out of the sink. Water the greens, being sure to aim the water directly at any remaining shells to fully moisten them.

Of course, avoid watering too much. Allow thirty seconds for the soil to soak up the water, then let any excess water drain away. If the tray isn't already leaning inside the sink, lift one end and rest it along the sink's top edge to promote drainage. After a few minutes, turn the tray around and allow it to drain from the other end too. With practice, you'll learn to gauge how much water is needed, and you may have little or no excess water to drain away.

Day 5, 6, or 7: Harvest the greens. The optimal time for harvest ends with the first sign of the second set of leaves, the true leaves. Be on the lookout for the appearance of these two tiny leaves in the center of the large seed leaves. Before the true leaves emerge, the microgreens will be sweet and tender, but they'll soon turn tough and fibrous. If you delay your harvest, your crop will be larger and taller, but also tough and tart.

Harvest the sunflower greens before the true leaves emerge and as soon as the leaves have cast off all or most of their shells. During the summer, when direct sunlight is plentiful, this could happen as early as the evening of day 4, but don't harvest before the morning of day 5. This allows the sunflower greens to metabolize their sugars and starches overnight. During the rest of the year, you can more realistically expect to harvest on the morning of day 6 or day 7.

If some shells still cling to the leaves, remove them before harvesting. Simply pluck off any remaining shells by hand. It's much more difficult to try to remove shells after harvesting.

If you plan to refrigerate the sunflower greens, don't water the greens from above the day before harvesting because the greens won't dry in time. If you must water, water from the side (see pages 47 to 48).

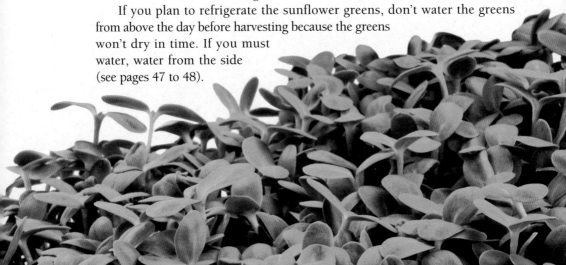

DAYS 5 TO 14: Watch the waves. Sunflower seeds will produce a second wave—and even third, fourth, and fifth waves—though each is sparser than the wave before. During the second wave, the greens can total more than one-third of the amount of the first wave, and they'll taste just as good. When the greens are grown in a cafeteria tray, the third wave will be less plentiful; by now, the nutrients in the soil will be depleted, making the crop far less palatable. The fourth and fifth waves will be stunted and inedible.

Since lack of nutrients in the soil is the problem, if you want to harvest all the waves of sunflower greens, you could add fertilizer to the seedling mix or potting soil before sowing the seeds. Another alternative is to use more seedling mix or potting soil in the first place, which means switching from shallow cafeteria trays to pint containers or seedling trays.

When growing sunflower greens in cafeteria trays, which hold only a thin layer of soil, harvest only the first and second waves, then toss the remaining mat of greens into your compost heap. Among the diurnal birds and nocturnal mammals who will savor the remaining waves of sunflower greens, none will register a complaint with the gardener.

PEA SHOOTS

The mature green peas of certain cultivars are used for growing pea shoots. You won't find these in the grocery store or even the natural food store; you must order these peas, or seeds, from garden seed suppliers. The favored cultivars of green peas for growing pea shoots include field pea, sugar pea, dwarf sugar pea, sugar pod pea, snap pea, sugar snap pea, and snow pea. Take note that flowering sweet pea (*Lathyrus odoratus*), an ornamental flower whose shoots are considered poisonous, *should not* be used to grow pea shoots.

Unlike sunflower seeds, peas need not be kept in the refrigerator. They can be stored at room temperature.

Grow Your Pea Shoots

Pea shoots are cultivated nearly identically to sunflower greens, but there are differences between the two. Sunflower greens thrive in heat, while pea shoots tolerate a wide range of temperatures. Lacking shells that must be shed, pea shoots demand less attention. And after their initial harvest, the second and third waves arise not from postponed germination but from subsequent cuttings of the same shoots.

The steps for growing pea shoots in cafeteria trays are roughly the same as those for growing sunflower greens. The following steps highlight the different requirements for growing pea shoots. Note that timelines for growing pea shoots won't be the same as those for growing sunflower greens.

SOAK THE PEAS. Just as you would soak sunflower seeds before sowing, you must soak peas for eight hours (but soaking them for twelve hours is even better if you have the opportunity to change the water midway through the soaking time). This step is especially important for peas because the viable ones swell during soaking but the dead ones don't. This means you can identify and remove the dead peas, which won't germinate and grow into shoots, before you sow them. If at this early stage you find there are too many dead peas to bother to remove, then proceed no further. Compost the entire jarful and the rest of your supply.

GERMINATE THE PEAS. Germinating the peas before planting isn't as critical as it is for sunflower seeds, but this step is still recommended. Depending on the cultivar, germination may take twice as long as for sunflowers.

PREPARE THE SOIL. Peas should be sowed in potting soil, not seedling mix. If you aspire to harvest second or third cuttings, add fertilizer to the soil. Alternatively, simply use more soil, which means switching from shallow cafeteria trays to pint containers or seedling trays.

SOW THE PEAS. Cover the peas with a thin layer of potting soil to ensure that the rootlets grow downward rather than helter-skelter. Any soil that sticks to the shoots as they emerge will wash off later since you'll be watering the shoots from above. The growth stage will again depend on the cultivar and may be twice as long as that for sunflowers. For the second wave of shoots, it may be longer still.

WATER FROM THE TOP. Top watering is recommended for the early stages of growth to ensure that the peas remain hydrated. If you grow pea shoots only

under indirect sunlight and in a room with stagnant air, mold might develop not on the stems or leaves, but on the peas themselves. With the first such sign, remove any infected peas and switch to side watering.

PROVIDE AMPLE LIGHT. Pea shoots don't require as much light as sunflower greens, but pea shoots still require light, so make sure they get plenty of it. Some microgreen farmers grow pea shoots in nearly total darkness to keep them tender and blanched. However, with scant leaves and lacking chlorophyll, such shoots fall short in both taste and nutrition.

HARVEST THE SHOOTS. When harvesting pea shoots, you can count on as many as three cuttings per tray. The number of cuttings is limited only by the depletion of nutrients in the soil. As nutrients are exhausted, growth rates slacken and sweetness decreases. But until the soil is depleted, successive cuttings of pea shoots don't diminish in quantity. As a result, peas can provide a good return on your investment if they're planted in fertile soil.

The first cutting can be harvested after nine or ten days if the pea shoots are grown in direct sunlight, even in winter. If the pea shoots have been grown in less intense light, count on two more days until the first harvest.

Before harvesting the shoots, inspect them closely. You should see a knob at the very bottom of the stem from which two tiny leaves barely emerge. Higher up the stem, you'll see the first set of full-grown large leaves. For the first cutting, snip the stems just above these large leaves if you intend to harvest a second or third cutting. On subsequent cuttings, snip higher up the stems. If your first cutting will be your sole harvest, snip the stems just below these leaves. Below that, the stems will be brittle and bitter.

Expect eight to ten days to elapse between each successive cutting. The optimal number of cuttings per tray depends upon the cultivar and vigor of the pea, the fertility of the soil, how high up the stem you snip, and how long you allow the shoots to grow between cuttings. The third cutting may not be as sweet, given that taste and nutrition diminish with each cutting. Also with each cutting, the distance between each cluster of leaves increases, resulting in longer stems and fewer and smaller leaves. After the third cutting, it would be a good idea to retire the tray of pea stubs to the compost heap.

Enjoy Pea Shoots Raw or Steamed

Pea shoots grow not only leaves but also tendrils, which taste as good as the leaves. New cultivars have been selectively bred to accentuate their tendrils, which are the feathery tips of the stems that serve as "hands." The tendrils reach for and grab onto immobile objects for support as the growing pea plant climbs.

Pea leaves and tendrils are delicious eaten raw and just as they are. The first two cuttings of peas deserve to be served as the sole ingredient of a plain, undressed salad. However, when they're cooked, pea shoots are quite sweet. For the best results, steam the shoots—even the leftover cooking water tastes good.

the inside scoop: sunflower and pea

SUNFLOWER

- Use unhulled black oil sunflower seeds to grow sunflower greens.
- Measure sunflower seeds before soaking. Try starting with ½ cup of seeds per cafeteria tray. Alternatively, determine the amount of seeds to plant by spreading a single layer of seeds in an empty tray. The seeds shouldn't touch each other.
- Soak sunflower seeds for eight hours before sowing, freshening the water at least once during that time.
- Germinate sunflower seeds in a sprouting jar for twenty-four hours before sowing, rinsing the seeds at least twice during that time.
- When it's time to plant, fill the cafeteria tray to the rim with moist soil, sow the appropriate amount of sunflower seeds for the size of the tray, and lay the seeds evenly and thinly upon the soil. Don't cover the seeds with soil; this is an exception to the general rule, as soaked seeds are typically covered with soil after sowing.
- Until the seeds germinate, cover the cafeteria tray with another tray. As the seedlings emerge, put some weight on top of the tray to encourage vigorous growth.
- Early in the growth cycle, use a spray bottle or mister to moisten the sunflower seeds and emerging seedlings. Switch to top watering when the seedlings are firmly anchored.
- If possible, put sunflower greens outside in direct sun before harvesting to help the leaves grow and shuck the shells.
- Harvest sunflower greens before the second set of leaves, or true leaves, appear. If necessary, pluck off any remaining shells by hand before harvesting.

PEA

- Use the mature stage of certain cultivars of green peas to grow pea shoots (buy these from a garden seed supplier).
- Soak peas before sowing. Ideally, also germinate them in a sprouting jar before sowing.
- Sow peas in potting soil, not seedling mix.
- Water peas from the top, but switch to side watering at the first sign of mold.
- Expect up to three cuttings of pea shoots per tray. Snip the stems above the large leaves if you plan on successive cuttings.

recommended microgreens

More than fifty species of microgreens are recommended because they're the most flavorful. In addition, the seeds tend to be affordable and the greens grow quickly. With only a few exceptions, the following microgreens take less than one week to germinate and less than two weeks to reach harvest length.

A great deal can be said about the unique qualities of each microgreen. To make the entries somewhat uniform, the following information is provided when it applies.

NAME: Vernacular names in American English are listed first. Enclosed in parentheses and italicized are the scientific names, which include the genus and species. (When "var." appears in the scientific name, it's an abbreviation for "variation.") Alternative, colloquial, or foreign-language names may also be listed.

Science is constantly evolving, and the scientific names for plants also change over time. In fact, the scientific community isn't currently in agreement about all plant names, and one authoritative list upon which all botanists agree doesn't exist. The primary sources for the scientific names used in this book are the books and websites listed under resources (see "Scientific Resources on Plants," page 100). Secondary sources are the seed packets, websites, and catalogs of several seed suppliers.

EASY OR DIFFICULT TO GROW: Essentially, the designation "easy to grow" means you have great potential for a successful harvest, and "difficult to grow" means you have an increased risk of crop failure. Each of the following microgreens is given one of four rankings: very easy, easy, difficult, and very difficult.

COOL- OR WARM-SEASON CROP: The term "cool season" refers to short days with weaker sunlight, while "warm season" means long days with stronger sunlight. Keep in mind that light and darkness affect the pace of plant growth more than warmth or cold.

Most of the following microgreens are designated as either cool-season or warm-season crops, but one or two excel in the hot season. Cool-season crops thrive below 65 degrees F (18 degrees C). In fact, cool-season crops create their plant sugars as a defense against the cold; for example, mature kale and apples turn sweet only after the first frost of fall. Warm-season crops thrive above 75 degrees F (24 degrees C), and some hot-season crops do well in even higher temperatures.

Despite these designations, once germinated, most microgreens will grow at room temperature, which is 65 to 75 degrees F (18 to 24 degrees C), unless otherwise stated below. All microgreens generally, and members of the genus *Brassica* especially, will grow at temperatures outside their labeled ranges; however, they won't grow as rapidly and their flavors may not be at their peak.

If you produce a crop with either a low yield or a bitter flavor, wait until the season changes and try growing it again. If you're still unsuccessful, wait for another change in season and try yet again.

SOAKING: Unless otherwise stated below, seeds need not be soaked before sowing.

SOWING: Unless otherwise stated below, seeds should be gently pressed into the soil but not covered with soil.

GERMINATION: Unless otherwise stated below, most microgreen crops, even cool-season crops, require temperatures above 70 degrees F (21 degrees C) to germinate quickly and at high ratios. This is the temperature at which the first radicles appear, and unless otherwise stated, the radicles emerge and achieve the same lengths as their seeds in 2 to 3 days.

Note that germination times as given on seed packets and in seed catalogs pertain to seeds that are planted outdoors. When seeds are sown outdoors under soil, it takes longer for the seedlings to emerge above the soil. In most cases, microgreen seeds are sown upon the soil, thereby reducing germination time by 2 days or more.

SUNLIGHT: Unless otherwise stated below, seedlings thrive under direct sunlight, so give them access to as much as the season provides.

HARVEST: Unless otherwise stated below, flavor and succulence vary little between the seed leaf and true leaf stages, so harvesting most microgreens can be optimal during either stage. Don't rely on the number of "days until harvest "that seed sellers may advertise. Accurate predictions are made impossible by the sheer number of variables that affect the pace of seedling growth. These include seed cultivar, seed vigor, soil fertility, soil acidity, water acidity, water purity, nighttime temperature, daytime temperature, day length, sunny or cloudy weather, and the list goes on. Plus, you must take into account the most variable factor of all: you. No one but you can say at what stage you best like the looks or flavor of any given microgreen.

While this range may be too broad to hold much meaning, microgreens can usually be harvested sometime between 1 to 4 weeks after sowing. If you'd like to make a rough calculation of time to harvest, you can base your estimate on the number of days to germination. If you count the days it takes for a seed to germinate and multiply that figure by 4, you'll have the approximate number of days that will elapse from the time the seeds are sown until the seed leaves peak (before the emergence of any sign of true leaves). Next, take that number and multiply it by 2 to get the approximate number of days that will elapse from the time the seeds are sown until the first true leaves fully unfold.

FLAVOR: Because they're so subjective, opinions about flavor and palatability may be much less meaningful than such distinctions as "easy to grow" and "difficult to grow." However, it may be helpful to know if the flavors of microgreens differ appreciably between the seed leaf and true leaf stages, and this information is provided below when applicable. Unless otherwise stated, flavors at seed leaf stage are nearly the same as those at true leaf stage.

CULTIVARS AND COLORS: Often, differences among cultivars are negligible with regard to microgreens, and no one cultivar may offer advantages over others within a species. But some cultivars really shine for their own specific characteristics, and in these instances, they're named accordingly.

When it comes to color, microgreen leaves are more or less green and stem colors are off-white or very pale yellow at harvest time. Exceptions are noted.

NOTES: Additional information that may be helpful is listed in this field.

Alfalfa *(Medicago sativa)*

EASY TO GROW.

WARM-SEASON CROP.

GERMINATION: Alfalfa germinates in 1 to 2 days.

SUNLIGHT: Protect alfalfa from direct midday summer sun.

NOTES:

- Some people may be concerned about growing alfalfa microgreens because alfalfa sprouts have been associated with food-borne illness. While any crop can be contaminated by animal-based fertilizers, alfalfa has proven an especially efficient carrier because the seeds' surface is scored to hasten germination, and the scoring provides a hideout for microbes. The conditions of warmth, moisture, and darkness necessary for sprouting provide the perfect environment for microbes to proliferate, and rinsing and stirring can spread microbes to uncontaminated sprouts. The process for growing microgreens doesn't include stirring, however, and the sunlight necessary for microgreen growth is a sanitizer that kills microbes that might be in the soil. Since side watering and bottom watering don't disturb the soil or cause it to splash on stems and leaves, you need not worry about the risk of eating tainted alfalfa microgreens (or any microgreen, for that matter) when these methods are used.

- Alfalfa microgreens (as compared to sprouts) grow large, green leaves. These leaves make the microgreens more nourishing and appetizing than the sprouts.

Amaranth *(Amaranthaceae family)*

Red Amaranth

VERY DIFFICULT TO GROW.

HOT-SEASON CROP.

SOAKING: Definitely *do not* soak amaranth seeds. If you do, they might not germinate at all.

GERMINATION: Amaranth germinates in 2 to 3 days if temperatures are above 75 degrees F (24 degrees C).

FLAVOR: There are two types of amaranth: one is cultivated for its grain and the other for its leaf. Microgreens are grown from leaf amaranth (which is called also Chinese spinach), and there are two types: red and green. The flavor of red amaranth is bland, but its intense color makes up for it. Don't bother to grow green leaf amaranth, as the color doesn't compensate for its lack of flavor.

CULTIVARS AND COLORS: At seed leaf stage, the very fragile leaves and stems of Red Garnet amaranth (*Amaranthus tricolor*) are a fluorescent and almost supernatural magenta. In fact, photographs of red amaranth show such intense color, you might suspect computerized enhancement when there's none. At true leaf stage, the color of red amaranth deepens to purple.

NOTE: Because amaranth microgreens are such a brilliant red at seed leaf stage, they're beautiful when mixed with other microgreens. The contrasting hues are quite striking.

Arugula *(Eruca versicaria var. sativa)*

NAME: In the Western Hemisphere, this salad green is known by its Spanish name, *arugula*. The British name is rocket, a corruption of its French name, *roquette*.

EASY TO GROW.

COOL-SEASON CROP.

SOWING: Do not soak or cover this mucilaginous seed.

GERMINATION: Does well in low temperatures.

SUNLIGHT: Arugula flourishes in indirect sunlight and shows sunburn when exposed to direct midday sun, especially in summer.

HARVEST: Because arugula is bitter at seed leaf stage, it's better to grow it to true leaf stage, although it may take a while for leaves to mature. The mucilaginous hulls tend to cling to the leaves.

FLAVOR: Tangy, similar to its close relative radish.

Asian Greens *(Brassica rapa)*

VERY EASY TO GROW.

COOL-SEASON CROP, but will usually tolerate warm and hot seasons.

GERMINATION: Most Asian greens germinate in 2 days, though seed suppliers state 7 to10 days.

FLAVOR: Most Asian greens provide a very mild mustard-like aftertaste, while others are neutral or bland. The greens are noted more for their nutrients than their flavors.

CULTIVARS AND COLORS:

- Altor *(Brassica rapa* var. *japonica)* is a hybrid of mizuna and kyona.
- Green or purple mizuna *(Brassica rapa* var. *nipposinica)* has green leaves or green leaves with purple veins. This microgreen provides a sizable second wave.
- Hon tsai tai *(Brassica rapa* var. *chinensis)* has green leaves and purple stems and tastes like radish.
- Red or green komatsuna *(Brassica rapa* var. *perviridis)*, also known as Japanese mustard spinach or spinach mustard,

Green Mizuna, Purple Mizuna and Komatsuna

Yukina Savoy

germinates in only 1 day during the hot season and 2 days during the warm season. It has deep purple leaves with green undersides or green leaves and thrives even in summer heat; it's a veritable year-round green. The mild mustard flavor at seed leaf stage sometimes gets stronger at true leaf stage; otherwise, this green remains mild.

- Yukina savoy (*Brassica rapa* var. *rosularis*), also called savoy, is similar in appearance and growth to napa cabbage but tastes like bok choy. This microgreen tolerates heat.

NOTE: A Japanese mustard green, mizuna belongs to two separate species, *juncea* and *rapa*. (See mustard greens, page 84, for mizuna in the species *juncea*.)

Basil *(Ocimum basilicum)*

DIFFICULT TO GROW.

WARM-SEASON CROP.

SOWING: Fill the soil to the rim because basil's stems are short and it grows low. Spread the seeds especially thinly and don't allow them to touch each other, since they're very mucilaginous and will congeal into a solid mass when first watered. Once the seeds are watered, don't disturb them.

Cinnamon Basil

GERMINATION: Basil seeds are difficult to germinate, but light enhances germination. If the seeds are kept in darkness, they'll still germinate, but at a low ratio initially, resulting in a sizable second wave.

HARVEST: Due to overcrowding, the seedlings hardly grow once the true leaves form, though they'll become more fibrous. Therefore, it's best to harvest basil before or just as the true leaves emerge. If initially germinated in darkness, basil yields a significant second wave, so wait for it after the first harvest.

FLAVOR: Both the seed leaf and true leaf stages provide the same distinctive mint-like flavor for which mature basil is known.

CULTIVARS AND COLORS:

- Cinnamon basil (*Ocimum basilicum* var. *cinnamomum*) has green leaves with purple veins and purple stems. Its cinnamon aroma is stronger at seed leaf stage, but even then you must poke your nose into the leaves to detect it. Despite its name, this microgreen doesn't taste like cinnamon, so these seeds may not be worth their extra expense to you.

- Lemon basil *(Ocimum basilicum* var. *citriodora)* germinates in 4 to 5 days, more slowly than other basils, and has bright green leaves and a pronounced lemony flavor (but less of a basil flavor). Its uniform growth causes the leaves to form a tightly woven, shield-like canopy. Of the five cultivars listed here, lemon basil is the most beautiful.

Purple Basil

- Opal or purple basil *(Ocimum basilicum* var. *purpurascens)* germinates in 2 to 4 days and has mostly purple leaves. Its flavor is bland compared to sweet basil, so grow this microgreen only for its color. Unlike other specialty basils, the seeds are relatively inexpensive. Because the germination rate is the same as for sweet basil, try growing the two together by mixing 1 part opal basil seeds with 10 parts sweet basil seeds.

- Sweet basil *(Ocimum basilicum* var. *basilicum)* germinates in 2 to 4 days. Its flavor is superlative and best before the true leaves begin to emerge. This is the cultivar that serves as the high standard by which all other basils are measured. Only Thai basil rivals its delicious flavor. Sweet basil seeds are far less expensive than other basil seeds; consider purchasing seeds by the pound (one-half kilo) since sweet basil will likely rank as your favorite microgreen despite its small yields and demanding cultivation.

Sweet Basil

- Sweet Thai basil *(Ocimum basilicum* var. *thyrsiflorum)* germinates in 4 or more days and has tiny, delicate, yellow-green leaves that turn green after 7 or 8 days. Stems turn rose-purple if exposed to direct light; if crowded, the stems on interior plants remain buff green. Thai basil grows more slowly and is smaller than sweet basil and even has a less plentiful second wave, which simply means that most of the seeds germinated during the first wave. Thai basil is sweet basil's only rival in terms of flavor. Its unique licorice flavor warrants its extra growing time and lower yield,

Thai Basil

though perhaps not its greater expense. Thai basil is the most expensive of the five cultivars listed here.

NOTE: Once you harvest basil microgreens, don't refrigerate or store them below 50 degrees F (10 degrees C) or the leaves will blacken and turn to mush.

Beet and Chard *(Beta vulgaris)*

NAME: Beet and chard are so closely related that they share identical Latin names.

VERY DIFFICULT TO GERMINATE BUT EASY TO GROW.

COOL-SEASON CROP.

SOAKING: Each beet or chard seed is actually a pod, and there are as many as 6 seeds inside each pod. Because the pod contains a substance that inhibits germination, soaking is required. Soaking the pods for just 2 hours dissolves the inhibitor, while soaking for 8 to 24 hours also softens the hard, armor-like pod and hastens germination by 2 days.

SOWING: Cover the soaked pods lightly with soil (this will further hasten germination). Keep the soil on the dry side, otherwise the roots won't penetrate it.

GERMINATION: When soaked and covered with soil, the pods will germinate in 4 days (rather than 6 to 7 days when not soaked or covered).

Beet

Chard

FLAVOR: When grown for 10 to 14 days, both beet and chard taste like mature raw spinach, which isn't surprising since all three are members of the same family. Beet has a stronger flavor than chard, and neither microgreen will appeal to everyone. Try them more for their color than for their flavor.

BEET CULTIVARS AND COLORS:

- Bull's Blood beet (*Beta vulgaris* var. *crassa*) has dark burgundy leaves and red stems and tolerates both heat and cold.
- Ruby Queen, Red Ace, and Early Wonder beet (Beta *vulgaris* var. *vulgaris*) have green leaves with red veins. Sometimes the leaves have red tints and the stems are red.
- Yellow beet (*Beta vulgaris* var. *vulgaris*) has green leaves with yellow veins and yellow stems.

CHARD CULTIVARS AND COLORS:

- Bright Lights or rainbow chard (*Beta vulgaris* var. *tricolor*) are varieties that have green leaves and red, yellow, and pink stems. They have a milder flavor than red chard.
- Golden, ruby red, and yellow chard (*Beta vulgaris*) have green leaves and red or yellow stems.
- Orange, red, or yellow Swiss chard (*Beta vulgaris* var. *cicla*) have green leaves with red or yellow tints and red or yellow stems.

Bok Choy *(Brassica rapa* var. *chinensis)*

NAME: Bok choy is also called pak choi.

VERY EASY TO GROW.

COOL-SEASON CROP, but tolerates warmth very well.

GERMINATION: Bok choy usually germinates in 2 days but may germinate in 3 days in very cool or very warm temperatures. Highest germination ratios occur at temperatures above 75 degrees F (24 degrees C).

SUNLIGHT: This microgreen thrives in full sun but can grow nearly as well in part sun and part shade.

FLAVOR: Mature bok choy is traditionally eaten cooked, so the flavor of the raw microgreen may be unfamiliar and challenging to you. Accept the challenge!

Da Cheong Chae Bok Choy

CULTIVARS AND COLORS: Among dozens of cultivars, the following grow the fastest and have arguably better flavors (spicy at seed leaf stage and milder at true leaf stage):

- Black Summer bok choy *(Brassica rapa* var. *chinensis* "Black Summer") has dark green (not black) leaves. As its name suggests, this microgreen, unlike most bok choys, can endure hot seasons. While summer heat doesn't enhance its growth rate, neither does it stunt it; however, avoid exposing this microgreen to midday summer sun because the leaves may get sunburned.

- Da Cheong Chae bok choy *(Brassica rapa* var. *chinensis* "Da Cheong Chae") has spoon-shaped true leaves that are similar to those of Rosette bok choy (tatsoi) and grows to a pleasingly uniform height. The flavor is probably the best among the many bok choys. Untreated seeds are in short supply.

Rosette Bok Choy (tatsoi)

- Kinkoh bok choy *(Brassica rapa* var. *chinensis* "Kinkoh") has bright yellow-green leaves. Its flavor is the mildest, so perhaps the most appetizing, among the bok choys.

- Red bok choy *(Brassica rapa* var. *chinensis* Red Choi) has green leaves with red fringe, which deepens and spreads across the leaf with exposure to cold.

- Rosette bok choy *(Brassica chinensis* var. *rosularis* or *Brassica rapa* var. *narinosa)* is the smallest bok choy and

Red Bok Choy

is usually called tatsoi (some horticulturists consider it a separate species, hence its distinct name). Unlike other bok choys, this microgreen doesn't tolerate warmth. In addition, its flavor differs from all other bok choys.

NOTE: Bok choy deserves center stage in any homegrown microgreen garden. It grows quickly, is very easy to grow, and is highly nourishing.

Broccoli *(Brassica oleracea var. italica)*

EASY TO GROW.

COOL-SEASON CROP, but tolerates warmth.

HARVEST: Harvesting this microgreen at seed leaf stage is recommended. Its disheveled appearance even at seed leaf stage is surprising among microgreens in the genus *Brassica*.

FLAVOR: Broccoli microgreens are only slightly more savory than the florets of fully mature raw broccoli.

CULTIVARS: Broccoli seeds that are marketed specifically for growing sprouts or microgreens rarely, if ever, are identified by cultivar, yet they typically equal or surpass lower-priced named cultivars both in vigor and flavor. Plus, they're sold in bulk and cost less than the named cultivars.

Broccoli

NOTE: While all *Brassica* microgreens contain very high levels of cancer-fighting phytonutrients, broccoli contains the most.

Broccoli Rabe *(Brassica rapa var. ruva)*

EASY TO GROW.

COOL-SEASON CROP.

GERMINATION: Broccoli rabe germinates at a high ratio when temperatures are above 75 degrees F (24 degrees C).

FLAVOR: The seed leaf stage is spicy-mustard hot, but the greens become milder at true leaf stage.

Broccoli Rabe

NOTE: Broccoli rabe has little in common with broccoli and is more like bok choy. It grows to a pleasing uniform height and is especially attractive compared to the disheveled discord of broccoli.

Cabbage *(Brassica oleracea* var. *capitata)*

DIFFICULT TO GROW, as compared to other *Brassicas.*

COOL-SEASON CROP, but also tolerates warmth.

GERMINATION: Cabbage germinates in 3 to 4 days and requires temperatures above 75 degrees F (24 degrees C) for a high ratio of germination.

CULTIVARS AND COLORS: The three main groups of cabbage are red, green (also called white), and savoy. Seeds for savoy cabbage *(Brassica oleracea* var. *sabauda)* are more expensive than green cabbage seeds; since the microgreens hardly differ, skip savoy cabbage.

- Green cabbage *(Brassica oleracea* var. *capitata* f. *alba)* is also called white cabbage. In fully mature cabbage, interior leaves are blanched white because exterior leaves block the sunlight; when this variety is grown as a microgreen, all the leaves are exposed to light and turn green. This microgreen may appeal only to raw-food enthusiasts.

- Red cabbage *(Brassica oleracea* var. *capitata* f. *rubra)* has deep red leaves and red stems or green leaves with red veins, red fringes, and red stems. The flavor is unappetizing, and no particular cultivars are recommended for superior taste.

Cabbage and Red Cabbage

NOTE: Unlike red cabbage, green cabbage fills the room with a mild cabbage smell as it grows, which can't be characterized as pleasant.

Carrot *(Daucus carota* var. *sativus)*

VERY DIFFICULT TO GROW.

WARM-SEASON CROP.

SOWING: Carrot seeds and seedlings are tiny, and this crop grows best in loose, granular soil and won't take root if the soil's surface is crusty.

GERMINATION: Carrots will germinate in 1 week when the temperature is 75 degrees F (24 degrees C), but germination takes longer in cooler temperatures.

Carrot

HARVEST: When no cultivar is identified, seeds sold specifically for carrot microgreens can be very slow growers. Out of sheer impatience, you'll likely want to harvest at four weeks regardless of leaf stage.

Chard *(see beet, page 70)*

Chervil

Chervil *(Anthriscus cerefolium)*

NAME: Chervil is also called garden chervil.

DIFFICULT TO GERMINATE AND GROW.

COOL-SEASON CROP.

GERMINATION: Chervil germinates in 10 to 12 days. It needs light and cold to germinate and prefers temperatures between 55 and 60 degrees F (13 and 15.5 degrees C).

SUNLIGHT: Chervil thrives under direct sunlight as long as it's not too hot; if it is, provide some shade. Sunlight promotes the growth necessary for the leaves to shed the long black hulls that otherwise cling to them.

HARVEST: Grow to true leaf stage until the leaves shed most of their hulls. While the hulls are soft and edible, chervil's texture is more appealing without the hulls.

FLAVOR: Similar to fennel, chervil tastes as good as the sound of its name suggests.

Chicory *(Cichorium intybus var. foliosum)*

DIFFICULT TO GROW.

COOL-SEASON CROP.

GERMINATION: Chicory germinates in 4 to 6 days at 60 degrees F (15.5 degrees C) and in more time (not less time) at higher temperatures.

HARVEST: This microgreen grows slowly, taking more than 3 weeks from germination to true leaf stage. Harvest at true leaf stage.

FLAVOR: Chicory's flavor is very bitter at seed leaf stage and less so at true leaf stage.

CULTIVARS AND COLORS: Chicory is cultivated for its dark green leaves with red spines and red stems.

NOTE: Don't confuse this chicory, which is cultivated for its leaves, with chicory root *(Cichorium intybus var. sativa)*, which is cultivated for its root.

Chives *(see onion, page 86)*

Chrysanthemum, Garland *(Chrysanthemum coronarium)*

NAME: This microgreen is also called edible chrysanthemum. In the West, it's known by its Japanese name, *shungiku*.

EASY TO GROW.

WARM-SEASON CROP.

GERMINATION: Chrysanthemum germinates in 8 to 10 days at temperatures of 60 to 65 degrees F (15.5 to 18 degrees C).

FLAVOR: Though a warm-season crop, it will turn bitter at temperatures above 75 degrees F (24 degrees C).

Cilantro *(Coriandrum sativum)*

NAME: Different parts of the cilantro plant are known by different names, and these vary by place. The seeds, ground as a spice, are called coriander. In Britain, Spain, and the Western Hemisphere, the leaves are known by their Spanish name, cilantro, and are eaten as an herb. Elsewhere, the leaves are called Chinese parsley.

DIFFICULT TO GROW.

WARM-SEASON CROP.

SOAKING: Soak the seeds for 8 to 24 hours to soften the hard hull and decrease germination by 2 days.

Cilantro

SOWING: Cover the seeds lightly with soil to ensure darkness and further soften the hard hulls, making it easier for the leaves to cast them off.

GERMINATION: When soaked and covered with soil, cilantro seeds germinate in 5 to 6 days; otherwise, they germinate in 7 to 8 days. Germinate in darkness and at temperatures below 70 degrees F (21 degrees C).

SUNLIGHT: Don't expose cilantro to direct sunlight during the first week after germination or its leaves will become sunburned. Direct sunlight is recommended during the second week, yet even then the hulls may still cling to the leaves.

HARVEST: Cilantro's signature true leaves don't fully develop until almost the third week; just for the sake of seeing their beauty, you might consider growing this microgreen to true leaf stage.

FLAVOR: Cilantro's flavor is more aromatic at seed leaf stage, but it's good at true leaf stage too, though sometimes slightly bitter. Some people find even the smell of cilantro repugnant, while others savor it.

Clover *(Trifolium)*

EASY TO GROW.

COOL-SEASON CROP.

GERMINATION: Clover germinates in 1 to 2 days and can germinate at temperatures as low as 40 degrees F (4.5 degrees C), although this may take 1 to 3 weeks.

SUNLIGHT: Protect from direct midday summer sun.

CULTIVARS AND COLORS:

- Crimson clover (*Trifolium incarnatum*) is also called Italian clover. "Crimson" refers to the color of the flower.
- Red clover (*Trifolium pratense*) is also called purple clover, and its flower can be either red or purple.

NOTES: Both clover and its close cousin alfalfa are fodder for farm animals. Since clover has a longer history as a plant food for humans, you might consider growing it rather than alfalfa. Alfalfa seeds, however, are more widely available, especially in natural food stores.

Cress

Cress, Garden *(Lepidium sativum)*

NAME: Cress is also called peppergrass.

DIFFICULT TO GROW.

COOL-SEASON CROP.

SOWING: Sow cress only in small batches because it doesn't store well and its flavor is so intense that a little goes a long way.

GERMINATION: Cress germinates in 1 to 2 days.

HARVEST: Multiple cuttings are possible if cress is first harvested past the true leaf stage.

FLAVOR: The spicy, hot-pepper flavor of cress is slightly milder at true leaf stage but still quite zesty. Use cress as a seasoning, just as you would use ground pepper.

CULTIVARS: All cress cultivars are suitable for microgreens. Persian cress (*Lepidium sativum*) is the mildest, and pepper cress (*Lepidium bonariense*) is the hottest.

NOTES:

- Don't confuse garden cress with watercress or winter cress.
- Garden cress was grown and eaten in England as a microgreen for many decades before the word "microgreens" was even coined.
- Cress is a most unusual *Brassica*: its seeds are mucilaginous, its leaves are uniquely shaped, its stems sustain multiple cuttings, and its odor fills the room.

Dill *(Anethum graveolens)*

DIFFICULT TO GROW.

COOL-SEASON CROP.

GERMINATION: Dill germinates in 7 or more days. It requires light and temperatures below 70 degrees F (21 degrees C) to germinate.

SUNLIGHT: Grow dill only when you can provide it with full sun; otherwise, it becomes very leggy.

FLAVOR: Dill is worth growing, despite the extra effort required, because of its delicious flavor.

NOTE: The microgreen seed is identical to dill seed that's used as a seasoning. You'll recognize them as the seeds used in making dill pickles.

Endive and Escarole *(Cichorium endivia)*

NAME: Endive and escarole are so closely related that they share the same Latin name.

DIFFICULT TO GROW.

COOL-SEASON CROPS.

SOWING: Since neither endive nor escarole develop a very long stem, fill the soil right up to the rim when growing these microgreens.

GERMINATION: Endive and escarole germinate in 2 to 4 days.

SUNLIGHT: Both microgreens grow well during the short days of winter sunlight without supplementary lighting. During summer, seek direct sunlight but avoid midday direct sunlight (but since both endive

Endive

Escarole

and escarole become fibrous and taste acerbic when grown in warmth, it's best to grow them only in cool weather). Be aware that mature commercial crops usually are grown in darkness during their last several days to decrease some of their bitterness. If you wish to grow these microgreens in darkness, do so only during the last 1 to 2 days before harvesting.

HARVEST: True leaf stage is less bitter than seed leaf stage but looks less graceful. It takes several weeks for endive and escarole to grow to true leaf stage.

CULTIVARS: Differences among cultivars are hardly detectable when they're grown as microgreens, so simply seek the least expensive seeds available.

- Endive (*Cichorium endivia* var. *crispum*) has curly true leaves and is slightly less fragile than escarole. It also fares better in warmth than escarole.
- Escarole (*Cichorium endivia* var. *latifolium*) has broad, flat true leaves and a slightly less bitter flavor than endive. It fares well in cool and even cold weather.

NOTE: These microgreens look so graceful, you can grow them in pint (one-half kilo) containers and offer them as gifts to your dinner host. Just don't be surprised if your host uses the beautiful microgreens as a centerpiece instead of harvesting and serving them.

Fennel, Leaf *(Foeniculum vulgare* var. *dulce)*

NAME: Fennel is also called sweet fennel.

DIFFICULT TO GROW, yet easy compared to other herbs in the Apiaceae family.

Fennel

COOL-SEASON CROP.

SOAKING: Soak fennel seeds for 8 to 12 hours to soften the hulls.

SOWING: Cover fennel seeds with soil, which both hastens germination and softens the hulls so the leaves can shed them more easily.

GERMINATION: Fennel germinates in 1 week, though seed suppliers state 1 to 2 weeks.

HARVEST: Harvest fennel 3 weeks after sowing, when the microgreen is still at seed leaf stage and the hulls still cling to most of the leaves. The hulls are quite flavorful and are soft enough to eat along with the leaves. While the feather-like true leaves are beautiful, they are not more flavorful than at seed leaf stage.

NOTE: Leaf fennel is cultivated for both its delicious leaves and seeds. Don't mistake it for Florence fennel (*Foeniculum vulgare* var. *azoricum*), which is cultivated for its stalk and swollen bulb.

Fenugreek *(Trigonella foenum-graecum)*

EASY TO GROW.

WARM-SEASON CROP.

SOAKING: Soak fenugreek seeds for 4 to 8 hours. The water will stain yellow, so try to change it after 2 to 4 hours.

SOWING: Fenugreek can be covered and weighted like sunflower or pea (see chapter 8). This is done not to ensure that the radicles take root but rather to promote thick, juicy stems. Maintain the cover and weight for 2 days after germination, then remove the cover and weight and expose the seedlings to light.

GERMINATION: Fenugreek will germinate in 2 days.

FLAVOR: Unless it's grown in darkness, the seed leaf stage is very bitter compared to the true leaf stage.

NOTES:

- Fenugreek seeds look like giant alfalfa seeds and grow like mung beans, which isn't unexpected since they all belong to the same legume family.
- Seek fenugreek seeds in the spice section of natural food stores.
- Suppliers of sprout or garden seeds market fenugreek seeds specifically for sprouting, but these seeds are just as suitable for growing microgreens.

Flax *(Linum usitatissimum)*

NAME: Flax is also called common flax or flaxseed, and its British name is linseed.

EASY TO GROW.

WARM-SEASON CROP.

SOWING: Flaxseeds are mucilaginous.

GERMINATION: Flaxseeds germinate in 3 days. Organically grown brown flaxseeds purchased fresh from natural food stores germinate at high ratios.

HARVEST: Harvest at seed leaf stage, when the flavor is better than that of true leaf stage.

CULTIVARS AND COLORS: The names of the two predominant cultivars, brown flax and golden flax, reflect the color of the seeds. Brown flax germinates at higher ratios, grows more rapidly, and tastes better than golden flax, so brown is the seed to seek.

NOTE: Flaxseeds and chia seeds share the same culinary qualities, but flax microgreens are far more tasty than chia.

Garlic Chives *(see onion, page 86)*

Kale *(Brassica oleracea var. sabellica)*

DIFFICULT TO GROW, compared to other *Brassicas*.

COOL-SEASON CROP, but tolerates some warmth.

GERMINATION: Kale germinates in 3 to 4 days.

FLAVOR: Kale microgreens have much the same flavor as mature kale when it's eaten raw. Cool temperatures enhance its sweetness.

CULTIVARS AND COLORS: Lacinato kale (*Brassica oleracea* var. *sabellica* f. *laciniato*), also called dinosaur kale, has dark green, almost blue, leaves. Its seeds are the least expensive, and it grows more quickly than all other kale cultivars.

Red Russian Kale

Kale, Red Russian
(Brassica oleracea var. acephala or Brassica napus var. pabularia)

EASY TO GROW.

COOL-SEASON CROP.

GERMINATION: Red Russian kale germinates in 4 days. It can germinate even at temperatures as low as 45 degrees F (7 degrees C), but this may take 8 or more days.

HARVEST: At true leaf stage, the leaves form the distinct petal shape that's so characteristic of mature red Russian kale. Just for its beauty, this microgreen is worth growing to true leaf stage.

FLAVOR: Kale microgreens have much the same flavor as mature kale when it's eaten raw. Cool temperatures enhance its sweetness.

COLORS: Cold turns the true leaves deep green and the seed leaves and stems reddish purple. Without cold, the leaves remain neutral green and the stems don't become red.

Kohlrabi *(Brassica oleracea* var. *gongylodes)*

DIFFICULT TO GROW, compared to other *Brassicas*.

COOL-SEASON CROP.

GERMINATION: Kohlrabi germinates in 4 days at temperatures above 75 degrees F (24 degrees C). It can germinate even at temperatures as low as 50 degrees F (10 degrees C), but this may take 3 weeks.

FLAVOR: Kohlrabi has a bland flavor when grown in warm temperatures and tastes more like radish when grown during the cool season. The flavor is better at the true leaf stage.

CULTIVARS AND COLORS: Purple kohlrabi has deep green leaves with a magenta tint and purple or magenta stems. It looks similar to red cabbage microgreens.

Lettuce *(Lactuca sativa)*

DIFFICULT TO GROW.

COOL-SEASON CROP.

SOWING: Lettuce grows shallow roots, so it need not be planted in deep soil.

GERMINATION: Lettuce germinates in 2 to 5 days, though seed suppliers often state 7 to 10 days. Lettuce germinates at the highest ratios when exposed to light and at temperatures below 70 degrees F (21 degrees C). Lettuce won't germinate at temperatures above 80 degrees F (27 degrees C).

SUNLIGHT: Avoid midday direct sunlight unless the greens are kept fully hydrated. Otherwise, most cultivars grow well in either sunlight or shade.

FLAVOR: Most lettuces turn bitter when grown during the warm season, so lettuce is best grown as a cool-season crop.

Green Romaine and Red Romaine

**Oak Leaf Lettuce and
Black-Seeded Simpson Lettuce**

CULTIVARS AND COLORS: Of the five broad groups of lettuce, romaine lettuce (also called cos) and leaf lettuce (also called looseleaf lettuce and including oak leaf lettuce) are best suited for microgreens. Romaine tolerates warmth and stands tall. Leaf lettuce grows quickly and spreads widely. The following are examples of varieties whose seeds are less expensive.

ROMAINE LETTUCES (*Lactuca sativa* var. *longifolia*):
- Outredgeous lettuce is the reddest of the red lettuces.
- Parris Island cos grows quickly but molds easily.

LEAF LETTUCES (*Lactuca sativa* var. *crispa*):
- Black-Seeded Simpson lettuce is the most popular leaf lettuce cultivar in part because it's highly tolerant of warmth.
- Red Salad Bowl lettuce is an oak leaf lettuce with excellent flavor, especially at true leaf stage. Its beautiful, multicolored red or purple leaves require cool temperatures and full sun for their color to fully bloom.

NOTE: Lettuce microgreens are very fragile and easily become damaged from mishandling, so they're seldom seen in the marketplace. Therefore, homegrown microgreens are quite a treat.

Marjoram, Sweet *(Origanum majorana)*

Sweet Marjoram

DIFFICULT TO GROW.

WARM-SEASON CROP.

SOWING: Fill the soil to the rim because marjoram's stems are short and it grows low.

GERMINATION: Marjoram germinates in 4 to 6 days. Light will enhance germination. Keep the soil relatively dry, or the tiny seeds will easily rot.

HARVEST: At seed leaf stage, marjoram tastes like mint. At true leaf stage, it emits an alluring aroma when it's cut. This crop produces a sizable second wave, just like basil.

FLAVOR: Because its flavor is so minty, you can grow marjoram to satisfy your longing for mint.

NOTE: Though sweet marjoram is a slow and finicky grower, it's worth growing even though it requires extra time and special care.

Millet *(Panicum miliaceum)*

EASY TO GROW.

WARM-SEASON CROP.

SOAKING: Soak millet for 8 to 12 hours. The very hard husk requires soaking.

SOWING: Grow in pint (one-half kilo) containers.

NOTES:

Millet

- Millet microgreens aren't grown for human consumption. Rather, they're grown as a treat for parakeets and hamsters, who savor millet in all forms. Don't snip the greens but simply put the container on the floor of the cage or habitat.

- Of the many species of millet, proso millet *(Panicum miliaceum)*, also called common millet, is the preferred millet microgreen of birds. Don't use Italian millet *(Setaria italica)*, whose British name is foxtail millet, or pearl millet *(Pennisetum glaucum)*, also called bulrush millet. These species have poor germination ratios, and their grasses are short and stunted compared to grass grown from proso millet.

- The parakeet seed you have been feeding your parakeet is unhulled millet that should germinate in high ratios, so try growing it. Millet for human consumption is hulled and germinates with poor vigor and at low ratios, if at all.

Mung Bean *(Vigna radiata)*

NAME: Outside of North America, mung beans are also called green gram.

VERY EASY TO GROW.

WARM-SEASON CROP.

SOAKING: Soak mung beans for 8 to 12 hours to decrease germination time.

SOWING: Mung beans can be covered and weighted like sunflower or pea (see chapter 8). This is done not to ensure that the radicles take root but rather to promote thick, juicy stems. Maintain the cover and weight for 2 days after germination, then remove the cover and weight and expose the seedlings to light.

GERMINATION: Mung beans germinate in 2 days.

HARVEST: Same as for fenugreek (see page 79).

NOTES:

- When purchasing mung beans from a natural food store, look for beans that lack wrinkles. Old and dry beans will result in decreased germination.
- Some people find mung bean microgreens more appetizing when they're grown in darkness. Professional growers may sell such microgreens, which are blanched white and labeled "golden."
- Mung beans are popularly grown as sprouts. The microgreens have straight, erect stems, also called shoots, that look more appealing than the usually jumbled sprouts. Once you grow mung beans as microgreens, you'll likely stop growing the sprouts.
- There are actually dozens of beans, such as chickpeas, haricots, lentils, and soybeans, that can be grown as microgreens in the same manner as mung beans. Fava and lima beans, however, should be avoided as microgreens because they may create a toxin soon after germination. Conversely, germination neutralizes the toxins found in other legumes.

Mustard Greens (Brassica juncea var. rugosa)

VERY EASY TO GROW.

COOL-SEASON CROP.

Red Giant Mustard

Purple Osaka Mustard

NAME: The *rugosa* variety of mustard greens is also called leaf mustard or Chinese cabbage mustard.

GERMINATION: Mustard greens germinate in 2 to 3 days, although seed suppliers state 7 to 10 days.

FLAVOR: Mustard greens have a spicy-hot flavor at seed leaf stage and are slightly milder at true leaf stage.

CULTIVARS AND COLORS:

- Garnet, Purple Osaka, Red Giant, or ruby mustard greens have green leaves with reddish-purple veins, deep green and deep red leaves, green leaves with a purple blush, or reddish-purple leaves with a reddish-purple blush. Cool weather is needed for the colors to deepen beyond green.
- Mizuna, a Japanese mustard green, belongs to two species, *juncea* and *rapa*. (See Asian Greens, page 67, for mizuna in the species *rapa*.)

NOTE: Mustard greens are very easy to grow throughout the year, making this microgreen an excellent choice for novices.

Mustard Seeds *(Brassica juncea* var. *juncea)*

Some mustard greens are cultivated for their seeds—which are used to make mustard, the condiment—and these seeds can be used to grow microgreens.

VERY EASY TO GROW.

COOL-SEASON CROP.

GERMINATION: Organically grown seeds from the spice section of natural food stores dependably yield very high germination rates.

HARVEST: These microgreens are fast growers and can be harvested in 1 week almost regardless of conditions and season. Harvest only the leaves, not the stems, where much of the heat is stored.

CULTIVARS AND COLORS:

- Black mustard *(Brassica nigra)* seeds disappeared from the marketplace and have been displaced by brown seeds because the brown seeds can be mechanically harvested, while the black seeds must be harvested by hand. The scientific name is sometimes erroneously applied to what is really brown mustard.

- Brown mustard *(Brassica juncea)* seeds, also called Indian mustard seeds, have outer hulls that are brown or reddish brown. Inside, the color is mustard yellow. As for the microgreens, the true leaves of some cultivars have a purple fringe and the stems are hairless. The flavor is spicy hot and truly mustard.

- White mustard *(Brassica alba, Brassica hirta,* or *Sinapis alba)* seeds are pale yellow or yellow-beige and are larger than most *Brassica* seeds. As for the microgreens, at true leaf stage, the leaves are larger than most *Brassica* leaves and are more like radish leaves. The stems are hairy. The flavor is spicy hot but *not* like mustard, so these microgreens aren't likely to please most palates.

NOTE: Serve mustard microgreens not as a side dish but rather sparingly as a garnish, the same as you would serve the condiment, which can be replaced by these microgreens. In fact, try drying the microgreens for long-term storage; when you're ready to use them, grind the dried greens and sprinkle them on top of dishes just as you would sprinkle ground pepper.

Napa Cabbage *(Brassica rapa* var. *pekinensis)*

NAME: Napa cabbage is also called Chinese cabbage.

Chinese Cabbage

VERY EASY TO GROW.

COOL-SEASON CROP.

GERMINATION: The cultivars listed below germinate in 1 to 2 days, but most others germinate in 2 to 4 days. This microgreen germinates easily with little regard to temperature.

HARVEST: Napa cabbage microgreens grow quickly and can be harvested within 1 week of sowing, regardless of season. Only radish and turnip microgreens grow faster.

FLAVOR: The delicate flavor of napa cabbage microgreens resembles the flavor of lettuce rather than cabbage. This green is sweeter at seed leaf stage, but you won't be disappointed by its true leaf stage.

CULTIVARS AND COLORS: Napa cabbage microgreens look beautiful with their distinctive yellow-green color; an accurate name for this shade is chartreuse. In warm weather, the leaves lose some yellow and become more green. With dozens of cultivars from which to choose, you may risk disappointment with any but the favored cultivars listed below, as most others have a mustardy edge.

- Kogane truly has the most pleasing flavor of all the many cultivars of napa cabbage. It tops the list of quick-growing microgreens with great flavors.
- Beka Santoh comes in at a very close second for flavor.

NOTE: Napa cabbage's distinctive bright yellow-green leaves add sparkle to any mix of microgreens with deeper green leaves.

Onion *(Allium)*

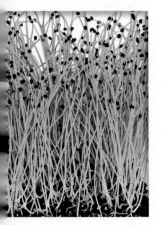

Onion

VERY DIFFICULT TO GROW at temperatures above 60 degrees F (15.5 degrees C).

COOL-SEASON CROP.

GERMINATION: Onions germinate in 1 to 2 weeks.

HARVEST: Onion microgreens can be harvested 3 to 5 weeks after sowing. Most leaves retain their hulls, but the hulls are small and soft enough to eat.

FLAVOR: Onion microgreens have the same intense, sharp flavor as their mature counterparts when eaten raw.

CULTIVARS AND COLORS:

- Bunching onions (*Allium fistulosum*) are also called scallions. The British name is Welsh onion.

- Chives (*Allium schoenoprasum*), also called onion chives, have hollow, tubular leaves. Don't confuse them with garlic chives.
- Garlic chives (*Allium tuberosum*), also called Chinese leeks, have solid, flat leaves like grass. When grown in light, the leaves are normally green; the white or yellow chives that are grown commercially are blanched by growing in darkness.
- Onions (*Allium cepa* var. *cepa*) have hollow, tubular leaves that look like pine needles.

NOTE: While mature onions usually emit odors only when cut, the seedlings have a distinct odor that fills the entire room in which they grow.

Orache *(Atriplex hortensis)*

NAME: Orache is also called orach or mountain spinach.

VERY DIFFICULT TO GROW.

COOL-SEASON CROP.

SOAKING: Soak orache seeds for 8 to 12 hours.

GERMINATION: Soaked seeds germinate in 7 days; germination takes longer if the seeds aren't soaked.

SUNLIGHT: Direct sunlight brings out the full purple or magenta color in these microgreens.

FLAVOR: Orache requires cool temperatures; otherwise, it will become very bitter.

CULTIVARS AND COLORS: Purple or magenta orache isn't well known in North America, but its seeds are widely available. Grow this microgreen for its color and mix it with contrasting green microgreens.

Pea, Garden *(Pisum sativum)*

NAME: Garden peas are also called field peas or green peas.

DIFFICULT TO GROW.

COOL-SEASON CROP.

SOAKING: Soak peas for 8 hours (or up to 12 hours, but only if the water is changed after 6 to 8 hours).

SOWING: Cover peas with soil to ensure that the radicles anchor securely.

Pea

GERMINATION: Peas germinate in 3 days at temperatures above 75 degrees F (24 degrees C), 4 to 5 days at 65 to 75 degrees F (18 to 24 degrees C), and 6 or more days at temperatures below 65 degrees F (18 degrees C).

SUNLIGHT: Protect peas from direct sunlight in summer. During other seasons, providing full sun all day is best, though a mix of partial sun and partial shade also produces good results.

HARVEST: Shoots can produce up to three worthy harvests, depending upon the quantity and fertility of the soil. Expect quick growth before the first cutting, slightly slower growth before the second, and even slower growth before the third. Refrigeration makes the stems fibrous, so try not to harvest more than you can consume at once. If refrigerated, the pea shoots are better cooked.

FLAVOR: Grown in cool temperatures, pea shoots are both sweet and succulent; grown in warmth, they lack sweetness; grown in cold, they lack succulence.

CULTIVARS AND COLORS:

- Snow pea (*Pisum sativum* var. *macrocarpon*) varieties include snap pea, sugar snap pea, and sweet snow pea.
- Sugar pea (*Pisum sativum* var. *sativum*) varieties include dwarf gray sugar pea (the seeds are gray), dwarf sugar pea, and sugar pod pea. For all three, the leaves have a reddish blush and the shoots have a reddish tinge.

NOTE: See chapter 8 for detailed instructions on how to grow pea shoots. (Growing pea shoots is roughly the same as growing sunflower microgreens.)

Purslane *(Portulaca oleracea var. sativa)*

NAME: Purslane is also called garden purslane and is closely related to an edible wild purslane.

EASY TO GROW.

WARM-SEASON CROP.

GERMINATION: Purslane germinates in 6 to 7 days in light and temperatures above 70 degrees F (21 degrees C). Otherwise, it takes 2 weeks to germinate.

CULTIVARS AND COLORS: Red or golden purslane has green or yellow leaves with pink or red stems.

NOTE: Popular during the nineteenth century, this leafy herb deserves renewed interest as a microgreen because of its unique, piquant flavor.

Radish *(Raphanus sativus)*

VERY EASY TO GROW.

COOL-SEASON CROP.

GERMINATION: Radish is the easiest and quickest of all seeds to germinate and of all seedlings to grow. It germinates in just 1 day (only turnip germinates as quickly), though some cultivars take 2 days. It can germinate at temperatures as low as 45 degrees F (7 degrees C), but then it takes 3 to 4 weeks to germinate.

SUNLIGHT: Direct sunlight is needed for the leaves to fully shuck off the hulls; however, the hulls are soft enough to eat, so don't be too concerned about either the full sun or the hulls.

HARVEST: Radish can be ready to harvest within 5 days of sowing regardless of growing conditions. Harvest it at seed leaf stage, because the stems become fibrous at true leaf stage.

FLAVOR: The flavor of this microgreen is similar to that of radish root but isn't quite as spicy and hot.

Radish

CULTIVARS AND COLORS:

- China Rose radish has green leaves and purple or rose stems.
- Daikon radish (*Raphanus sativus* var. *longipinnatus*) has green leaves and white stems, is the mildest of all radishes, and contains more vitamin C than any other microgreen.
- Hong Vit radish has dark green leaves and pink or purple stems.
- Red radish has purple-green leaves.

NOTE: While radish can grow in both warm and cold weather, cool temperatures color the stems with deeper reds.

Rutabaga *(Brassica napus)*

NAME: Rutabaga is also called Swedish turnip.

EASY TO GROW.

COOL-SEASON CROP.

HARVEST: Rutabaga's seed leaf stage lingers long, probably because of overcrowding, so be content if this microgreen never reaches true leaf stage.

COLORS: Rutabaga has reddish-tinged stems.

NOTE: *Brassica napus* also includes canola (or rapeseed), which shouldn't be grown as a microgreen even though it sometimes appears on lists of recommended microgreens. Rutabaga has a bland flavor, but canola's flavor is caustic.

Sesame *(Sesamum indicum or Sesamum orientale)*

Sesame

VERY EASY TO GROW.

WARM-SEASON CROP.

GERMINATION: Sesame germinates in 1 day. Organically grown seeds purchased fresh from natural food stores germinate at high ratios. Be sure to purchase unhulled sesame seeds, which are beige and chalky, not hulled sesame seeds, which are white and oily, as hulled sesame seeds won't germinate.

HARVEST: Harvest at the advanced seed leaf stage (7 to 10 days), just as the true leaves begin to emerge, because sesame is bitter at the early seed leaf stage and fibrous at the later true leaf stage. Stems are bitter regardless of leaf stage, so cut just below the leaves when harvesting.

CULTIVARS AND COLORS: There are two predominant types of sesame seeds. The first is smaller and black, and the second is larger and beige or buff. Seek the beige seed, as it germinates faster, grows faster, and tastes better.

NOTES:

- Unlike all other microgreens, sesame leaves retain their firmness when briefly steamed or lightly sautéed and have a better flavor when cooked.
- At seed leaf stage, sesame leaf is among the most beautiful of microgreens; its form is reminiscent of flower petals.
- Sesame originates in Africa and India. For centuries, both the leaves and the seeds have been consumed for their medicinal qualities.

Sorrel

Sorrel *(Rumex acetosa)*

DIFFICULT TO GROW.

COOL-SEASON CROP.

GERMINATION: Sorrel germinates in 4 to 5 days at temperatures below 65 degrees F (18 degrees C) and 5 to 6 days at higher temperatures.

HARVEST: The sweetness of the seed leaf stage diminishes by the third week, so harvest early.

FLAVOR: Beautiful and delicious, but little known, sorrel is greatly underappreciated. Its flavor combines both the sourness of citrus and the sweetness of sugar, much like lemonade. The unique flavor comes through even when sorrel is mixed with other microgreens that taste either bitter or bland.

CULTIVARS AND COLORS: Red-veined sorrel (*Rumex sanguineus*) has green leaves with red veins; only some leaves have subtle red tinges.

Spreen *(Chenopodium giganteum)*

NAME: Most North Americans will be unfamiliar with spreen, which is known in Britain as tree spinach, goosefoot, lamb's-quarters, or magenta spreen.

DIFFICULT TO GERMINATE, but easy to grow.

WARM-SEASON CROP.

GERMINATION: Spreen germinates in 12 to 14 days at temperatures above 70 degrees F (21 degrees C) and when exposed to light. In darkness, germination may take up to 3 weeks.

HARVEST: Spreen is a slow grower. Even 4 weeks after sowing, it can be barely tall enough to cut for harvest.

Spreen

FLAVOR: Spreen's flavor is similar to raw spinach, but it's grown more for the alluring red blush on its leaves and upper stems than for its flavor.

CULTIVARS AND COLORS: Look for magenta spreen.

Sunflower *(Helianthus annuus)*

EASY TO GROW, but difficult to germinate and nurture to take root.

WARM- OR HOT-SEASON CROP.

SOAKING: Soak sunflower seeds for 8 to 12 hours to hasten germination by 24 hours and soften the seeds' shells.

SOWING: Sprouting in a jar or sprouting container before sowing is recommended to further soften the shells.

GERMINATION: Sunflower germinates in 2 days with soaking and 3 days without.

Sunflower

SUNLIGHT: Provide direct sunlight.

HARVEST: Harvest at seed leaf stage. If the true leaves begin to emerge, harvest immediately.

FLAVOR: Sunflower has a unique flavor but loses succulence and flavor when grown in cool temperatures.

CULTIVARS AND COLORS: Black oil sunflower seeds, not striped sunflower seeds, are preferred. Black refers to the color of the seeds' shells, not to the greens. Sunflower greens that are grown in direct sun have deep green leaves and very short stems. Greens that have had ample sunlight display green, not blanched white, stems.

NOTE: See chapter 8 for detailed instructions on how to grow sunflower greens.

Turnip

Turnip *(Brassica rapa* var. *rapa* subvar. *pabularia)*

VERY EASY TO GROW.

COOL-SEASON CROP, but also fares well in warmth.

GERMINATION: Turnip germinates in 1 day at temperatures above 75 degrees F (24 degrees C) and rivals radish in its speed and ease of both germination and growth. It can germinate at temperatures as low as 45 degrees F (7 degrees C), but then germination takes 1 week.

SUNLIGHT: During warm seasons, turnip grows better with partial shade, especially during midday.

HARVEST: Harvest at seed leaf stage, because turnip microgreens become fibrous at true leaf stage or even at seed leaf stage past two weeks.

CULTIVARS AND COLORS:

- Purple Top Globe turnip is *not* recommended for growing microgreens. This cultivar's flavor is bland at seed leaf stage and unpleasantly bitter at true leaf stage, when its flavor is nothing at all like that of the roots for which it's usually grown. Don't be lured by the low price of this seed.

- Seven Top turnip is one of several subvariations of *pabularia* that are recommended for growing microgreens. It's cultivated not for its roots but for its leaves, which are green with reddish veins and stems. The microgreen tastes just like the raw mature root.

Wheat *(Triticum aestivum)*

Wheat

VERY EASY TO GROW.

COOL-SEASON CROP.

SOAKING: Soak the seeds for 8 to 12 hours.

SOWING: The seeds can be sprouted in a jar or sprouting container for 1 day before sowing to confirm that the batch is viable.

GERMINATION: Wheat germinates in 1 to 2 days after the seeds have been soaked for 8 hours.

SUNLIGHT: Protect from direct midday summer sun.

CULTIVARS AND COLORS:

- Hard red winter wheat is widely acclaimed as the best for growing wheatgrass, and hard red spring wheat is a very close second. Red refers to the slight tint of the kernels, not to the color of the wheatgrass. When sold for growing wheatgrass, the wheat may be described as seeds, berries, or kernels.

- Spelt *(Triticum aestivum* var. *spelta)* is a relative newcomer to North America and produces a uniquely flavored wheatgrass that's worth trying.

NOTES:

- See chapter 8 for detailed instructions on how to grow wheatgrass.
- While any whole grain, such as barley, oat, or rye, can be grown into grass, wheatgrass is simply the sweetest.
- Unlike greens that are eaten directly, wheatgrass is grown to be juiced (or chewed to extract its juice).
- Cats and dogs like wheatgrass too. Grow and serve it in pint (one-half kilo) containers to satisfy your companion's natural craving for fresh greens.

Red Russian Kale

10

recipes

To savor the flavor of microgreens, you need only one "recipe": pick up a cluster of just-harvested microgreens, pop it in your mouth, and chew. Concentrate on the taste and texture of every fresh, raw, and unadorned morsel.

You'll digest microgreens better when you chew them fully and eat nothing else with them. Of course, some microgreens are too spicy or hot to be eaten in this manner. These include cress, mustard, and onion, which can be mixed with milder greens or added sparingly, like a condiment, to other dishes.

For variety, microgreens can also be enjoyed salad-style with a light dressing, or they can be used to top vegetable dishes as a healthy finish. The following recipes include other ideas too, such as incorporating them in appetizers or stirring them into cooked but slightly cooled dishes, where they'll wilt but maintain their integrity.

In general, microgreens shouldn't be cooked, but pea shoots and sesame microgreens are the exceptions. They hold up to heat, and their flavor even improves with cooking. Other microgreens, however, dissolve to mush when cooked, so keep this in mind if you like to be creative in the kitchen.

NOTE: The following recipes indicate the number of cups of microgreens required. One cup of microgreens, lightly packed, is the approximate yield of one pint container.

Facing page: Sweet Thai Basil, Purple Basil, and Sweet Basil

fennel RICE BALLS

The earthy flavor of brown rice pairs perfectly with fennel microgreens in this stunning and delicious dish. Soaking the rice first will cause it to germinate, which increases its nutritional value and makes it more digestible. Serve the rice balls along with your favorite sweet or salty dipping sauce.

2½ cups (591 milliliters) **water**

1 cup (237 milliliters) **short-grain brown rice** or **sweet brown rice**

½ cup (118 milliliters) **fennel microgreens,** harvested at seed leaf stage, lightly packed

3 teaspoons (15 milliliters) **chia seeds** (optional; see note)

3 tablespoons (45 milliliters) **black sesame seeds**

Put the water and the brown rice in a medium sauce-pan and soak for 12 hours at room temperature; do not drain. Bring to a boil over high heat. Decrease the heat to low, cover and simmer for 40 minutes, until the water is absorbed and the rice is tender. Fluff with a fork and transfer to a medium bowl. Let cool until comfortable to handle but still warm.

Harvest the microgreens by cutting just below the joint where the two leaves meet. Chop or dice the microgreens.

To make the rice balls, stir the microgreens into the warm rice until the greens are slightly wilted. Stir in the optional chia seeds to make a firmer ball. Scoop about 2 rounded tablespoons of the mixture and roll it between your palms to form a 1½ inch-wide ball. Repeat with the remaining mixture. If you've added the chia seeds, let the balls sit for 10 minutes to firm up.

Put the sesame seeds on a plate. Roll each rice ball in the seeds until it's coated.

Put the balls on a large plate and refrigerate until firm, about 1 hour. Serve chilled.

NOTE: If you use sweet brown rice, you don't need to add the chia seeds because this type of rice is naturally firm and sticky. If you use short-grain brown rice, including the chia seeds will make the rice balls firmer so they'll hold their shape better.

PEA SHOOT AND PEPPER *sauté*

YIELD: 4 SERVINGS

Red vegetables beautifully complement the vibrant green of most microgreens. When cooked, however, many red veggies lose their vibrant color. Not so with red bell peppers, which pop in this simple but eye-catching dish.

2 small **red bell peppers,** stemmed, seeded, and cut into chunks

2 tablespoons (30 milliliters) **coconut oil**

4 cups (about 1 liter) **pea shoots,** lightly packed (see note)

Put the bell peppers and the oil in a wok or large skillet. Cook over high heat, stirring occasionally, until the bell peppers are tender-crisp. Stir in the pea shoots and cook, stirring frequently, for 1 to 2 minutes. Serve immediately.

NOTE: Four cups of pea shoots, lightly packed, is the approximate yield of two pint containers harvested after two weeks.

MICROGREEN *medley*

This colorful salad showcases the deep green of bok choy, the yellow-green of napa cabbage, and the red of radish and red Russian kale. These cool-season crops thrive under the same growing conditions and make a zesty wintertime salad. In fact, the cooler the temperature, the darker and more brilliant the red Russian kale microgreens will become. Serve this medley with your favorite vinaigrette to harmonize the flavors.

1 cup (237 milliliters) **bok choy microgreens,** harvested at seed leaf stage, lightly packed

1 cup (237 milliliters) **endive microgreens,** harvested at true leaf stage, lightly packed

1 cup (237 milliliters) **napa cabbage microgreens,** harvested at seed leaf stage, lightly packed

1 cup (237 milliliters) **red radish microgreens,** harvested at seed leaf stage, lightly packed

1½ cups (355 milliliters) **red Russian kale microgreens,** harvested at true leaf stage, lightly packed

Put all the microgreens in a large bowl. Toss gently. Serve immediately.

POTATOES *and greens*

Cooked potatoes and beets make a delicious combination, and the same can be said for potatoes and beet greens. Since beet and chard are very closely related, either chard or beet microgreens can be used in this recipe. And think of fingerlings as "micro" potatoes!

16 to 20 **fingerling potatoes**

2 teaspoons (10 milliliters) **dried dill weed, dried basil,** or **dried parsley**

¼ cup (59 milliliters) **hempseed oil** or **flaxseed oil**

1 cup (237 milliliters) **red Swiss chard microgreens** or **red beet microgreens,** lightly packed

Preheat the oven to 350 degrees F. Lightly oil a baking sheet.

Put the potatoes on the prepared baking sheet and bake for about 50 minutes, until browned. Let cool until comfortable to handle.

Cut the potatoes into halves or quarters. Sprinkle with the dill weed and oil, then toss gently. Add the microgreens and toss gently once or twice, so most of the greens remain on top of the potatoes.

RESOURCES

MICROGREENS SEEDS AND NEEDS

For a downloadable list of vendors who sell seeds and supplies (such as trays and lighting) for growing microgreens, refer to the author's website: markbraunstein.org/growmicrogreens.htm.

SCIENTIFIC RESOURCES ON PLANTS

Some microgreen gardeners may want to dig into books and websites that are quite detailed about the unique characteristics of a given genus and species. Such resources can be instructive to curious chefs and erudite gardeners who are perplexed by the similar appearance yet unique tastes and diverse traits of many seeds and seedlings.

Books

Food Plants of the World by Ben-Erik van Wyk

This book is a succinct reference with one page devoted to each of 354 species of plants.

The New Seed-Starters Handbook by Nancy Bubel

This fertile source of information about germinating seeds and growing seedlings provides many solutions that other books lack. This classic remains as relevant today as when it was published in 1988.

Websites

Catalogue of Life: catalogueoflife.org

Integrated Taxonomic Information System: itis.gov

International Plant Names Index: ipni.org

The Plant List: theplantlist.org

USDA Plants Database: plants.usda.gov

GLOSSARY

Brassica. *Brassica* is a genus of plants in the mustard family that includes broccoli, cabbage, and kale. Many species that are grown as microgreens belong to this large genus.

Chlorophyll. Chlorophyll is the green plant pigment involved in photosynthesis and the marker of healthy microgreens.

Cotyledon. See "Seed leaves."

Cultivar. Specific varieties of a single species of a cultivated plant are called cultivars.

Hydroponics. The method of raising plants in nutrient solutions (fertilizer and water) instead of soil is called hydroponics. Adaptations of the basic hydroponics technique include aeroponics (constant misting), bioponics (underwater aquaponics for plants), and vermiponics (systems using compost tea and worm castings).

Mucilaginous. Seeds that when moistened are sticky or have sticky secretions are referred to as mucilaginous.

pH. The measure of acidity or alkalinity in a solution, pH is represented by a numerical scale in which seven is neutral, with lower numbers indicating acidity and higher numbers indicating alkalinity.

Photosynthesis. Photosynthesis is a process that occurs in green plants that transforms light into plant matter.

Phytonutrients. Phytonutrients are compounds derived from plants that provide health benefits to animals who consume them.

Polyethylene. Polyethylene is a type of lightweight plastic used in food packaging. Some forms (polyethylene terephthalate, PET, PETE, or recycling number 1) are less stable and more likely to migrate into food under certain conditions than other forms (high-density polyethylene, HDPE, or recycling number 2).

Radicle. The radicle is the embryonic seedling root that emerges as a seed germinates.

Seed leaf stage. The seed leaf stage is the stage during which the first set of leaves, or seed leaves, are seen growing on a seedling.

Seed leaves. Seed leaves are the first paired set of leaves to emerge. Seed leaves are also referred to as cotyledons.

True leaf stage. The true leaf stage is the stage during which the second set of leaves, or true leaves, are seen growing on a seedling.

True leaves. True leaves are the second paired set of leaves to emerge. The name refers to the fact that plants begin to display their true characteristics at this stage.

INDEX

Page references for sidebars, scientific names of plants, and recipe names appear in *italics*.

Book Publishing Co.

books that educate, inspire, and empower

To find your favorite vegetarian and healthy-living books online, visit:
www.BookPubCo.com

Sprouts

Kathleen O'Bannon, CNC

978-1-55312-026-1 • $11.95

Sprout Garden

Mark M. Braunstein

978-1-57067-073-2 • $12.95

**Mushrooms
for Health and Longevity**

Ken Babel, CN

978-155312-047-6 • $11.95

The New Enlightened Eating

Caroline Marie Dupont

978-0-92047-083-1 • $19.95

Kombucha Rediscovered

REVISED EDITION

Klaus Kaufmann, DSc

978-0-92047-084-8 • $12.95

**Raw Food Made Easy
for 1 or 2 People**

REVISED EDITION

Jennifer Cornbleet

978-1-57067-273-6 • $19.95

Purchase these health titles and cookbooks from your local bookstore or natural food store,
or you can buy them directly from:

Book Publishing Company • PO Box 99 • Summertown, TN 38483 • 888-260-8458

Please include $3.95 per book for shipping and handling.